HANDBOOK

By
Alan Williams

© Alan Williams 2011
First Published RYA 2011

The Royal Yachting Association
RYA House, Ensign Way, Hamble
Southampton SO31 4YA
Tel: 0844 556 9555
Fax: 0844 556 9516
E-mail: publications@rya.org.uk
Web: www.rya.org.uk
ISBN: 978-1906435-264
RYA Order Code: G83

Totally Chlorine Free · Sustainable Forests · EMAS

A CIP record of this book is available from the British Library.

Note: While all reasonable care had been taken in the preparation of this book, the publisher takes no responsibility for the use of the methods or products or contracts described in the book.

Technical Editor: Mike Hart
Cover Design: Velveo Design
Typesetting: Velveo Design
Proofreading and indexing: Alan Thatcher
Printed: in China through World Print
Photographer: Alan Williams
Illustrations: Pete Galvin

Acknowledgements

We are all a product of those who have influenced our lives, events in our lives and our motivation to use what we learn in effective ways.

I have been fortunate enough to work and be inspired by some outstanding sailing people over the past 30 years; to name a few, Stephen Park, Chris Gowers, Kirsty Bonar, Brian Staite, Rob Wilson, Graham Vials, Jim Saltonstall, Issy Hutchinson, Ollie Green, Tim Hall, Mike Hart, Andrew Wills, Jonny McGovern, Richard Stanley, Kenneth Andreason, Hamish Wilcox, David Howlett, Ian Clingan, and Josh Metcalfe. Thanks too to Race Officers Adrian Stoggall, David Campbell-James and Peter Saxton, and Jury members including Sally Burnett, Chris Watts and Peter Fitt.

Special thanks to Duncan Truswell, RYA Youth Manager, Alan Olive, former RYA Coaching Development Manager and Dr Ben Chell, RYA Psychologist, who have helped to create a great coaching environment.

I would also like to thank Mike Hart, RYA Coaching Development Officer and former Flying Fifteen World Champion, for being the technical editor of this book and the coaches who shared their ideas with me including GBR Zone Squad coaches and Cardiff Optimists led by Nick Sawyer. Finally, thanks to Sarah, James, Kate and Jen.

Contents

20 years ago I met Alan on the slipway at Plas Menai National Watersports Centre. He was about to assess my performance at the conclusion of a RYA Instructors Course. I was at the time working at the centre where Alan was Chief Instructor, and is now Head of Centre.

With a thorough understanding of the coaching philosophies of all the outdoor pursuits governing bodies of the time, Alan would always have a number of suggestions of how to get a point across. There was room to develop your own style, provided the course satisfied the goals of the customers, and as long as it was safe!

This depth of influence is reflected in the breadth of advice between these covers.

I'm sure Bill Endicott (North American Kayak Slalom Coach) wasn't the first to coin the phrase "fascination with the process". Throughout days working alongside Alan, discussing coaching matters through long (occasionally too long!) evenings, searching for improvement, or the solution to a particular problem, this fascination is always evident. Once again the fruits of this endeavour are on these pages.

Perhaps because of the success of the GBR Optimist Worlds team in 2003, Alan has had a busy diary coaching Optimists, but the broad background and fascination with the process has allowed Alan to work seamlessly at all levels of the RYA's coaching scheme. Although titled as an Optimist Coach Handbook, everything in the book (with perhaps a little adjustment) is applicable at all levels, with a great framework for any coach to review their work and refine their technique. I'll certainly be pushing any keen young coach, seeking to improve, in this direction.

I hope you will all enjoy the read, improve your coaching, get fascinated, and be repeatedly rewarded by helping Optimist sailors improve their skills.

Chris Gowers
GBR Olympic Laser Coach

Welcome to the RYA Optimist Coach Handbook.

Helping young people to develop their sailing skills is great fun and provides a real sense of achievement. It's important to remember that for many youngsters their first steps afloat in an Optimist lead to a lifetime of enjoyment of the sport of sailing.

The Optimist is the first rung on the sailing ladder. They are sailed from a very young age up to the age of 15. Sailors then move on to the youth classes up to the age of 18. Post 18, they become a senior level sailor, either following the performance Olympic classes pathway or sailing in the many other non-Olympic classes.

It takes time to nurture a young sailor and one thing we know for certain is that every sailor develops at a different rate. Some sailors achieve great things in an Optimist and for others success comes at youth level and beyond.

Behind every Optimist sailor is a keen and enthusiastic family who need to be fully involved in their sailor's development.

This book will explore coaching, learning models, goal setting, mental toughness and how to run coaching sessions, and then move on to look at useful techniques, exercises and games to help you develop an Optimist sailor's skills.

We will cover some details of the techniques needed to sail an Optimist; however, for more specific detail, you need to read the RYA Optimist Handbook G44.

As you progress in your coaching skills you will acquire your own individual style and go on to develop your own favourite exercises and games, so be creative and have fun.

Alan Williams
Caernarfon

This book is dedicated to the parents and volunteers from IOCA (UK) who make Optimist sailing possible and my mother who made it all possible for me.

COACHING

The basics

In this section we'll take a look at what coaching is all about. It's not always that easy to define, but we can all spot a good coach when we see one. There are many ways to coach and there are lots of techniques and each coach is a unique individual. However, one thing unites all good coaches and that is their passion and enthusiasm. We will see that coaching is a cross between an art and a science; the aim is to help the sailors reach their competitive potential.

What is sailboat coaching?

It is widely recognized that there are a number of key components to coaching sailing.

Put simply, sail coaching is:

- Helping sailors to improve their performance and achieve their potential.
- Developing the sailor as an individual, not just the technical, tactical, physical and psychological aspects of sailing.
- Creating the right environment for a sailor to train and perform in.
- Providing direct instruction when required.
- Setting goals and putting in place steps which enable a sailor to achieve those goals.
- Accelerating the learning process by using a range of coaching techniques enabling sailors to learn new skills more quickly than if they weren't coached at all.
- Analysing and evaluating the outcomes.
- Helping the sailor to become independent.
- Motivating and enthusing sailors and most of all, it's all about having fun.
- Allowing the coach to develop as a coach and an individual.

So what is a coach?

To be able to coach successfully you need to be able to take on a variety of roles, and these include;

- **Instructor** – the ability to instruct basic and advanced techniques and be able to pass on information.
- **Communicator** – you need excellent communication skills, both verbal and non verbal, enabling you to get the best out of the sailors, parents and other coaches.
- **Motivator** – being positive and creating the right environment for a sailor to develop and to have the ability to help a sailor cope with the highs and lows of competition.
- **Psychologist** – helping a sailor develop confidence, take control of their learning, set realistic goals, develop commitment, and improve concentration.
- **Friend** – be supporting and helping the sailor through the successes and disappointments of training and sailing competition.
- **Manager** – includes programme planning, organising sessions and competition.
- **Historian** – knowing why things are as they are now, and how the sport has developed.
- **Learner** – you need to have a curious mind and a desire to learn new skills and keep up-to-date.
- **Technologist** – a knowledge of the boats, rigs, sails, foils and sailing equipment.
- **Scientist** – to leave no stone unturned, be prepared to solve problems and evaluate outcomes.
- **Guardian** – you may well find yourself responsible for a group of sailors. If you are, you need to think about their welfare, safety and development.
- **Ambassador** – you will be acting as an ambassador for the sport of sailing and will be expected to uphold the values of the sport.

Qualities of a good coach

To be a good coach you need to develop some positive personal qualities. Those listed below are high on any good coach's list of important qualities.

US Olympic Coach Bill Endicott coined the phrase – coaching is about a 'fascination with the process', leaving no stone unturned in the pursuit of reaching potential.

Coaching – an art or a science?

Coaching is a cross between an art and a science. The art is you and your approach and the science includes the tools you use to help you coach. Skilful coaches are constantly developing their skills and knowledge to help sailors develop and reach their goals; leave no stone unturned in your coaching!

Coach or instructor?

A question often asked is 'what is the difference between a coach and an instructor'? Instruction is a part of the overall coaching process. There are times when being instructed 'how to' and being given routines and drills is important. Often when working with beginners or improver level sailors there will be a high level of instruction. If you are working with a group of sailors for an extended period of time you will be able to coach those sailors for longer term development and the coaching process will most certainly include some instructing.

Coaching styles

All coaches develop their own styles of coaching. There are a number of styles which can be used and often the most successful coaches use different styles in different situations. The 4 interchangeable styles which I like to use are Inform – Discuss – Agree – Enable. The following illustration identifies the 4 styles and you can consider when it is appropriate to use them.

InfoRm

- Coach decides what to do
- Sailor not involved in decision
- Coach tells sailor what, how and when to do something

Discuss

- Coach decides what to do
- Coach explains what to do to sailors
- Coach asks questions to confirm understanding
- Coach tells sailor what to do and how to do it

Agree

- Coach and sailor outline training needs
- Coach and sailor discuss suggestions and ideas
- Coach and sailor decide what to do
- Coach and sailor decide what, when and how to do it

Enable

- Sailor outlines training needs
- Sailor outlines training conditions
- Sailor works up a solution
- Sailor and coach discuss what, when and how to do it
- Coach supports sailor doing activity

Coaching toolbox

You will learn and become skilful using a wide range of coaching techniques. Like all toolboxes you need to keep your tools sharp. This book will provide you with a wide range of tools to use, and it's your job not to let them go rusty!

Communication

Effective communication is essential when coaching sailing and later on in the book we'll look at some simple techniques to help you become an effective communicator.

Child development

Before starting to coach children it is essential you have at least a basic understanding of child development and *fig 1* will help.

fig 1

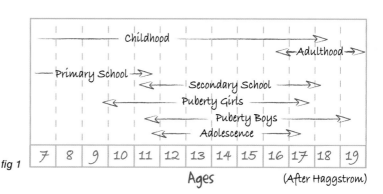

Child development timeline

It is important to note that while there are recognisable stages of child development it affects boys and girls differently and there is no exact time scale for when changes will take place. For example: a boy with a chronological age of 12 may be several years ahead of or behind another boy of the same age in terms of his biological or psychological age; this applies between girls as well. What matters is that you are aware of the individual differences between children of the same age and to take this into account when coaching.

Olympic Gold Medallist athlete David Hemery wrote a world class book called 'How To Help Children Find The Champion Within Themselves'. It's an easy read and essential reading for all coaches and parents.

Growing children

Children grow up a lot during their Oppy years, from young children taking their first steps afloat to unruly 14 to 15 year olds who will challenge everything you say. As they grow they need to adapt the way they sail the boat and your role as a coach is to help the sailor adapt their technique.

■ Girls usually start to mature between the ages of 12-14 and are fully developed by 15-16.

■ Boys on the other hand start their growth spurts later than girls, between 15-16 and are normally fully grown by the age of 18.

Boys have the classic mood swings and changes in behaviour, and in girls the development of menstrual cycles and how to cope with them needs to be taken into consideration.

During growth spurts some sailors lose coordination because bones grow faster than the surrounding muscles. Sailors often suffer from classic growing pains during growth spurts and so need support and reassurance.

Most parents will be aware of a growth spurt because clothing and footwear no longer fit and need to be replaced!

Coaching boys and girls

Both sail Optimists and do go on to be very successful at sail racing. It goes without saying that boys and girls are different and often have different needs.

Here are some ideas about coaching boys and girls:

- Boys usually mature later than girls and are usually stronger.
- Boys often like to get stuck in, while girls often like to think about it before doing something.
- Boys often respond well to more assertive language whereas girls will respond better to persuasion.
- Often boys are very competitive, they want to win and have to learn how to lose. Often girls need to learn about competing and winning.
- Girls often reach intellectual maturity earlier than boys.
- Girls can often concentrate for longer than boys.
- Girls are often more capable of multi-tasking (doing more than one thing at a time) than boys.
- Girls often show emotion, and boys often hide emotion.
- Girls often want to talk about what they are doing and boys don't – not to their parents anyway!

So when you are coaching boys and girls you need to be aware of the individual differences and integrate this into your coaching.

LEARNING

The most important thing you must learn as a coach is to recognise that you can't learn for the sailor. It's the coach's role to provide sailors with the opportunity to learn new techniques and help to develop sailors' skills. This section will focus on a variety of techniques you can use to help sailors learn. It is up to you to use these techniques to help in your coaching.

The brain, memory and recall

First of all we'll take a brief look at the brain and how it contributes to the learning process.

There are two halves or hemispheres to the brain, the left brain and right brain. In a simplified way each side of the brain has a range of functions. The left side of the brain deals with logic and the right side of the brain is the emotional side. Your job as a coach is to recognise that both halves of the brain are needed to harness its full potential. Children who are overly emotional need to be helped to use more logic in their decision making and sailors who are very logical need to access the more creative side of their brains.

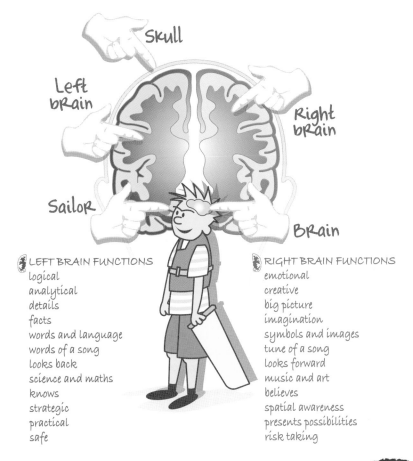

LEFT BRAIN FUNCTIONS
logical
analytical
details
facts
words and language
words of a song
looks back
science and maths
knows
strategic
practical
safe

RIGHT BRAIN FUNCTIONS
emotional
creative
big picture
imagination
symbols and images
tune of a song
looks forward
music and art
believes
spatial awareness
presents possibilities
risk taking

'Behaviour – it's a choice.' Dr Ben Chell, RYA Psychologist

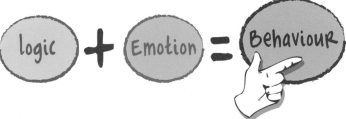

logic + Emotion = Behaviour

Memory and recall

Memory is both short term and long term. Material in the short term memory only transfers into the long term memory after a lot of practice.

If you are highly motivated you are more likely to remember something and it is more likely to be stored in your long term memory. Remember, things stored in the long term memory will fade or go rusty if you don't keep using them.

The memory game

We can all usually remember between 3-5 things from a theory session and often (if we are lucky) just 1-2 might be retained for longer! Check this by trying a simple experiment. Run a simple theory session, and then about half an hour later play the memory game (but don't tell the sailors that's what you are going to do).

Run a five question quiz based on the theory session, then get everybody to write down the answers. You may be surprised by just how few answers the group have remembered. The results may lead you to consider, in the future, simplifying sessions, whether land based or on the water.

Key words

You should be clear with the technical words you are using and what they mean. This will ensure a common language.

- **Technique** – the physical movements combined together to make up a sailing manoeuvre such as a tack or bearing away around a mark.

- **Pressure** – putting a technique under pressure by doing it faster / longer when distracted, or while trying to work out new priorities.

- **Motor skill** – for example the ability to tack and bear away around a mark.

- **Cognitive skill** – intellectual skills which need thinking about such as tactics and strategy.

- **Perceptual skill** – the ability to interpret information.

- **Skilful** – the ability to tack or gybe to a high standard consistently in varying conditions while under pressure – as in a race, or the ability to make the correct tactical decision based on the information available.

- **Closed skill** – an action which is internally self paced such as a tack or a gybe.

- **Open skill** – a skill which is affected by an unstable environment such as starting, sailing upwind in a group of boats or rounding a mark.

- **Pressure** – internal or external factors which may affect a sailor's performance.

Technique + Pressure = Skill

Skills development

To accelerate the learning process to help sailors develop and reach their potential you need to have really good coaching systems in place. The following ideas are designed to help you think about the way in which you coach.

Becoming an expert

- It is often said that it takes about 10,000 hours or about 10 years to become an expert in anything. (After Ericsson 1993)

- If it takes 10,000 hours or 10 years to become an expert, you have a lot of work to do, because even after 10 years there will be plenty of other experts to compete against.

- 10,000 hours is 20 hours per week, 50 weeks a year for 10 years. This is just about impossible to achieve in sail boat racing so you need to help accelerate the learning process.

Stages of learning

There are several models which cover the stages of learning. One of the simpler models developed by Fitts and Posner in 1967 still works well today. It identifies that there are 3 stages a sailor will go though in becoming skilful and adapted in their sailing.

1 – Beginner – Cognitive state

This stage takes a lot of mental effort while the sailor learns new movements and then has to apply them. It is often helpful for beginners to learn things in bite sized chunks, to prevent them from becoming overloaded either physically or mentally.

2 – Improver – Associative state

At this stage the sailor starts to make more progress, linking movements together more consistently with new techniques.

3 – Expert – Autonomous state

The expert is able to use appropriate techniques and use them consistently to a high standard in a wide range of environments without having to think about them. This enables the sailor to think about more strategic or tactical aspects.

Approaches to developing skills

Traditional methods

The traditional approach to developing skills is to create exercises, drills and routines, which are used to help a sailor develop good technique. This approach can work well in the short term and is often used to develop the technical aspects of sailing such as boat handling skills, speed, starting, mark rounding etc. However, these traditional methods don't always lend themselves to developing independent thinking skills and the tactics and strategy involved in sail boat racing.

Games for understanding

Another approach to developing tactical and strategic skills within sport which applies well to sailing is Teaching Games for Understanding (TGfU) which was developed by Rod Thorpe and David Bunker in 1982. This approach has been used in mainstream sports coaching for many years and can be applied to sail boat coaching. I have adapted the principles of TGfU for sailing.

Remember, make games fun

Decision making

The games are designed to enable the sailors to develop their tactical and strategic skills; the games are not just activity for the sake of activity. Sailors have to work out what to do, how to do it and when to do it.

Game form

Following a warm up, sailors participate in a game, which is designed for a particular learning point which can be any aspect of tactics or strategy.

Game appreciation

Sailors really need to understand what they are trying to achieve when competing.

Tactical awareness

Sailors must develop tactical options in a dynamically changing environment.

Skill

Sailors need to be able to perform manoeuvres as required – be skilful.

Does the game challenge?

The game needs to challenge the sailors.

Scoring

There are various ways to score the game: normal race scoring, marks out of 5 or 2 points for the boat which starts next to the start boat and one point for the best start.

Learning outcomes

It's not just a game, what are the learning outcomes?

Show me

Let the game ask the questions. You can try to use 'show me', rather than 'tell me'. However 'show me' can be used for technical stuff but is more challenging to demonstrate tactics in a sail boat race.

It depends

The common answer to questions is 'It depends'. Chris Gowers, Head GBR Olympic Sailing Coach, is renowned for using this phrase as it forces the sailor to recognise that often there are no simple answers to tactical questions.

RYA Skills Development Model

Over a number of years the RYA has developed and adapted a Skills Development Model which is a really useful coaching tool. The RYA Skills Development Model complements the Teaching Games Model because it acts as a set of tools when playing the game.

It works on 4 levels of competency, making it easy to identify which stage a sailor has achieved within each area of activity.

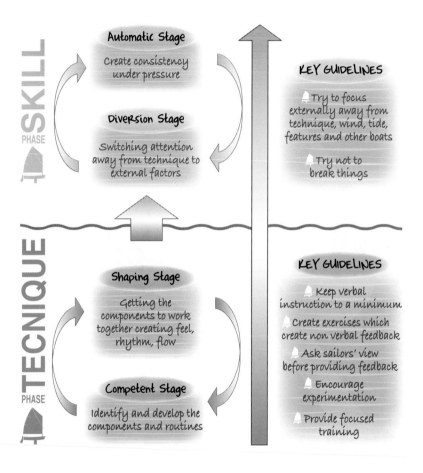

SKILL PHASE

Automatic Stage
Create consistency under pressure

Diversion Stage
Switching attention away from technique to external factors

KEY GUIDELINES
Try to focus externally away from technique, wind, tide, features and other boats

Try not to break things

TECNIQUE PHASE

Shaping Stage
Getting the components to work together creating feel, rhythm, flow

Competent Stage
Identify and develop the components and routines

KEY GUIDELINES
Keep verbal instruction to a minimum

Create exercises which create non verbal feedback

Ask sailors' view before providing feedback

Encourage experimentation

Provide focused training

Coaching tactics and strategy in sailing competition has always been challenging for coaches. This is due to some of the following reasons:

- The coach cannot communicate with sailors whilst they are racing.
- The race course is large and the coach is not able to see all the tactical decisions made by the sailors.
- The race course is dynamic and ever changing due to wind, weather and current.

Many of the exercises, routines and games used in sail boat coaching are designed to help sailors develop their own independent decision making skills, and a coach must develop activities to enable that process or the activity may be enjoyable to do but not help the sailor to understand the tactics and strategy of sailing.

 Think about how you will break down specific techniques and skill development when setting up games and exercises.

Mental imagery and rehearsal

Just as sailors might look at a video clip of themselves performing on the water, they can also use their brains to get a mental video clip of themselves performing. This can be a very powerful way of accelerating the learning process. Before events sailors can also use mental rehearsal to help them focus on their priorities and be ready for competition.

Learning styles

As individuals we all tend to prefer to learn something new in slightly different ways. The Learning Styles Model was developed by Honey and Mumford (1982) and identifies that there are 4 main learning styles, so let's take a look at them and apply the model to sailing.

1 – The Activist

Sailors who just jump in and have a go. They like to learn by doing it themselves and often keep doing it until they master it or give up!

2 – The Reflector

Often waits at the back and needs a lot of demonstrations and confirmation before having a go.

3 – The Theorist

We don't get too many theorists in sailing but when we do, they need multiple explanations and detailed discussion about how to do something before they will have a go. You may hear yourself saying 'don't worry about that, just have a go'.

4 – The Pragmatist

"It seems to work so that's good enough for me; I'll have a go" is the trade mark of the pragmatist.

In practice most people appear to be a mix of all of these styles and good coaching always includes explanations, demonstrations, and practical activity.

Self awareness and learning to learn

One of the critical skills is that a sailor understands themself. The more self aware a sailor is about their behaviour and how it impacts on their day-to-day life and sailing the better.

It is helpful if sailors know that they are attempting to learn new skills and techniques; this is because they will then have a better understanding of how they go about the process of learning, which in turn will accelerate the learning process.

Skilful learners usually understand the following:

1 – How they prefer to learn and their learning strengths.

2 – How they can motivate themselves and have the self-confidence to succeed.

3 – What they should consider, for example the importance of fluid intake, nutrition, sleep and a positive environment for learning.

4 – Some of the specific strategies they can use, for example to improve their memory or make sense of complex information.

5 – Some of the practices they must develop, such as reflecting on their learning so as to improve next time.

Don't prevent the learner from learning

When coaching it can sometimes be frustrating when a sailor isn't making the progress you think they should be. Remember that you can't learn for the learner. Your role is to help them to learn for themselves and help them overcome any particular obstacles.

How do we learn the nuts and bolts - VARK?

A complementary approach to the learning styles inventory is the VAK model originally developed by Bandler and Grinder in 1979. The R was added to make VARK by Fleming and Mills in 1992. VARK considers the four main ways that learners like to learn. We'll take a look at them.

Visual - Auditory - Read/Write - Kinaesthetic

Visual Learners

Like to learn by watching others, seeing demonstrations, video clips, diagrams and pictures. They also often understand patterns.

Auditory Learners

Like explanations and verbal confirmation – talking it through, lectures and taking notes.

Read/Write Learners

Like to read books and manuals to learn what needs to be done.

Kinaesthetic Learners

Like to get out there and do it – experiments, games and exercises. They learn by feel, touch and their senses.

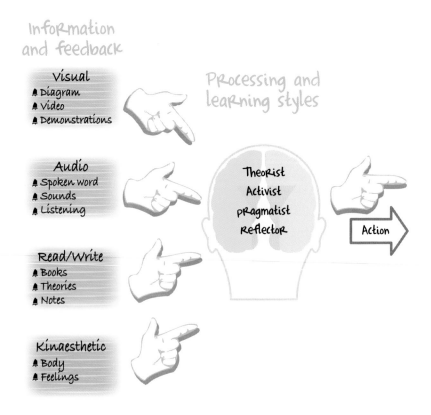

Information and feedback

Visual
- Diagram
- Video
- Demonstrations

Audio
- Spoken word
- Sounds
- Listening

Read/Write
- Books
- Theories
- Notes

Kinaesthetic
- Body
- Feelings

Processing and learning styles

Theorist
Activist
Pragmatist
Reflector

Action

It is possible to complete VARK questionnaires online which help identify a sailor's learning preferences.

In practice most sailors use a mix of all these learning styles. However, especially with young sailors there can be extreme results and some young sailors are very visual or kinesthetic. Often older sailors have learnt to learn using all the learning styles. Sailors need to understand their own learning style and learn also to use those which are less familiar to them. Coaches need to be aware of the sailors' learning styles and adapt their coaching accordingly.

There is a well known learning styles saying, which is simple and as powerful today as it was when it was written many years ago.

I hear and I forget
I see and I remember
I do and I understand

Digestible chunks

It is essential not to overload the sailor with too much information or try to get them to concentrate on too much at once. I like the following analogy:

'You wouldn't try to eat an elephant whole because you would get indigestion. You would need to break it down into small digestible chunks.'

Breaking down techniques

One of the main roles of a coach is to help learners learn. To do so you must think about the coaching methods you will use.

Some techniques are simple and easy for the sailor to learn and some will be more complex and take more time to learn. Simple techniques such as sheeting in or slowing down are often easily learnt by the sailor having a go at the whole activity. More complex techniques such as tacking or gybing are best learned using the whole-part-whole method. This involves breaking down a technique into its component parts and then linking them together to complete the whole technique.

Shaping is used to develop skill gradually over a period of time, an example would include tacking in light, medium and strong winds, and chaining is used to break down a complex technique into its components and then build them back up again.

An example of the whole-part-whole method in sailing is:

1 – The sailor views a demonstration or video of a particular technique, for instance a tack so that they see and understand how it should be done.

2 – Do some land drills to develop the movements needed to complete the tack, breaking down the tack into the components, and building it up again into the whole tack.

3 – Go on the water with the sailor and practise the tack.

4 – While on the water, work on no more than one or two elements at a time.

5 – Over a period of time, help the sailor in developing and refining their technique.

Experienced sailors

The whole-part-whole technique works well at a more advanced level to help correct or develop particular components of technique. You need to be aware that if you are using this surgical approach and focusing on one particular element, the sailor's level of skill performing the whole technique may deteriorate while the focus is on that one element.

Barriers to learning – self awareness

A coach is always aiming to accelerate the learning process, however there are many barriers to learning and sailors need to develop self awareness of how to manage them.

Frustration

Everybody at times gets frustrated even in sailing. Causes of frustration include not progressing as fast as the sailor would like, not understanding something, not achieving a race result or parents being frustrated at a lack of progress.

Frustration reveals itself in many ways. The most common are:

- Blame the equipment

  Always a great temptation to blame the equipment; it must be its fault!

- Blame someone or something else

  It couldn't be the sailor's fault, so they blame someone or something else.

- Sulk

   The sailor goes off and won't talk to anyone.

- Boredom

   Bored and can't see the point of the activity.

The cure

Sailors needs to recognise that everyone gets frustrated. Make them take a break, discuss what's wrong and find a way forward. Some sailors are successful in using a key word or phrase to bring themselves back into the here and now.

Making progress

Learning to be skilful takes time, and making progress is not just a straight line curve on a graph. What often happens is that progress will be made and then the sailor reaches a plateau in performance which may last some time. It is even possible for a sailor to appear to regress for a while. There is no exact science to this; the job of a coach is to try to narrow down the plateau and accelerate the learning process, enabling the sailor to make steady progress.

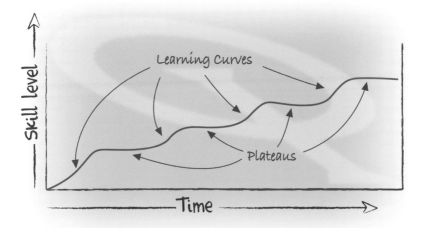

Overload and the catastrophe curve

One of the causes of hitting a plateau or even appearing to regress is overloading the sailor with either too much information or emotionally. It is essential not to overdo it; the following (after Hardy and Fazey 1987) illustrates this point:

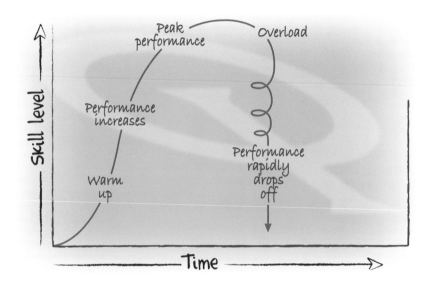

Self awareness and comfort zones

Encourage sailors to think about how they sail when they feel comfortable, and then about how they sail when they are anxious and stressed.

RYA Psychologist Gemma Douglas recommends the following coping and awareness strategy when a sailor gets out of their comfort zone.

Remember the more experience a sailor has the bigger their comfort zone will be.

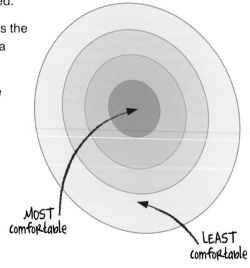

 Sailor Recognises that they are getting anxious/stressed

 Sailor presses the 'STOP' button in their head

 Sailor Refocuses on things they can control

Re-Learning

Sometimes you meet a sailor who has learnt to do something which isn't technically correct. To make progress the sailor needs to undo what they have learnt and re-learn the technique to make further progress. It can be quite a challenge to help a sailor undo what they have learnt; it's better to learn correctly to start off with.

A word of caution here though. Sometimes, a sailor will develop an interesting way of doing something which works well for them. In these cases you need to decide whether their technique will inhibit them from making progress, or to accept that it works for them and leave it alone.

Praise and learning from failure

One of the most important roles of coaches and parents is to help a sailor develop confidence. There has been a lot of research in this area and it is widely recognised that it is important to praise effort, and not results. That's not to say that we shouldn't celebrate success, just don't overdo it!

Too much praise of success can lead to fear of failure which often leads to poor performance. Coaches, parents and sailors need to see failure or setbacks as a natural part of the learning process and learn as much from it as possible.

PLANNING & GOAL SETTING

Planning and goal setting are important elements of the coaching process. In this section we will take a look at the detail behind how to plan and what goes into goal setting.

Planning

If coaching a group of sailors over a period of time you will need to consider the long term development of your sailors. The following techniques will help you with sailors' long term development.

Goal setting

This helps the coach and sailor understand what they are trying to achieve. It is generally recognised that there are 3 main types of goals. These are:

1 – Dream Goals

These tend to be longer term inspirational goals, for instance to emulate sailors like Ben Ainslie, Paul Goodison, Sarah Ayton or Iain Percy.

2 – Performance Goals

These are about achieving a performance such as winning a race or a competition. It is important to set realistic and achievable goals, because trying to achieve the unachievable can de-motivate and affect the confidence of a sailor.

3 – Process Goals

These deal with improving aspects such as technique, tactics or mental toughness. They can be used to break down complex techniques like tacking, gybing, mark rounding.

SMARTER goals

A useful tool to help manage goals, below is an example of how goal setting can be used to develop tacking skills.

Letter	Meaning	Using Smart Goals to develop tacking
S	Specific	Lean forward out of the tack and swap hands cleanly.
M	Measurable	Number of times done correctly out of 5. Use video to identify success.
A	Attainable	This is an achievable task.
R	Relevant	The sailor can already sail and has developed some bad habits which need to be corrected.
T	Time phased	Should be completed within 2 hours, and tested at the next session.
E	Exciting	Use a variety of exercises and games, use the skills model.
R	Reviewable	Debrief with sailor during and after session, video playback will help sailor.

Optimist skills matrix

Provides the coach and sailor with a useful tool to measure overall progress. A simple traffic light system is used to identify and measure current performance.

Needs a lot of attention

Needs some attention

Just needs maintaining

Tacking	Flat Water	Choppy Water	Tidal	Improvement Goal
Light Wind				
Medium Wind				
Strong Wind				
Step Tack				
Hop Tack				
Strap to Strap Tack				

Gybing	Flat Water	Choppy Water	Tidal	Improvement Goal
Light Wind				
Medium Wind				
Strong Wind				

Mark Rounding	Flat Water	Choppy Water	Tidal	Improvement Goal
Light Wind				
Medium Wind				
Strong Wind				
Laylines				

Goal Setting Dartboard

A useful tool, complete one at the beginning of training and another one at the end of a training period to see the progress a sailor has made.

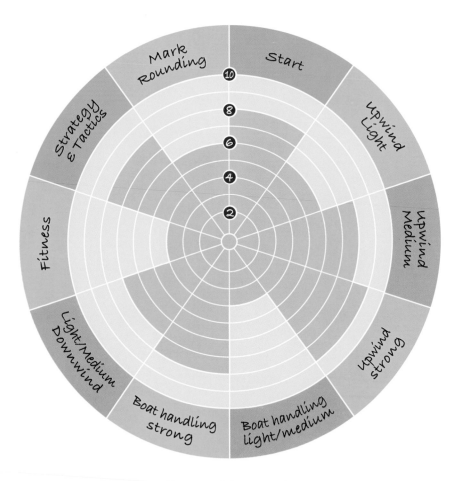

The Spider's Web

Sailing Diary

Every time a sailor goes sailing, a sailing diary should be completed, which will act as a record and reflection of the sailing session.

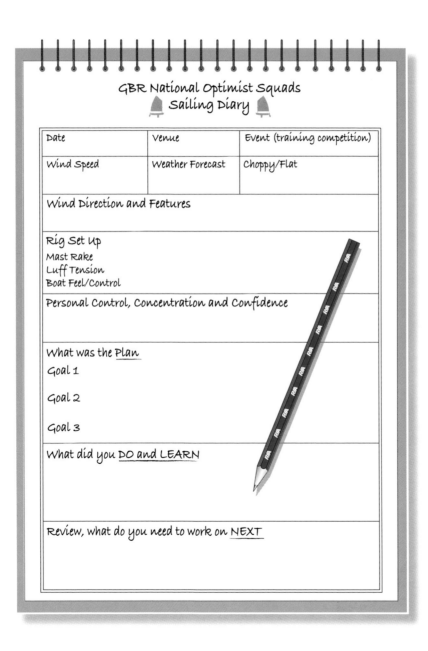

GBR National Optimist Squads
Sailing Diary

Date	Venue	Event (training competition)
Wind Speed	Weather Forecast	Choppy/Flat

Wind Direction and Features

Rig Set Up
Mast Rake
Luff Tension
Boat Feel/Control

Personal Control, Concentration and Confidence

What was the Plan
Goal 1

Goal 2

Goal 3

What did you DO and LEARN

Review, what do you need to work on NEXT

BASIC PSYCHOLOGY & MENTAL TOUGHNESS

Sailors must be able to cope with the pressures of competing in sail boat racing. Even the most skilful sailors will not win a race if they are stressed out.

One of your coaching roles is to help sailors to develop mental toughness.

There are a few simple techniques you can use to help a sailor develop mental toughness. The 5 Cs and 2 Rs are a simple way of thinking about mental toughness. The following shows how it can help to develop mental toughness.

This simple model has been developed by RYA Psychologist Dr Ben Chell and is a framework for a sailor to develop mental toughness.

Confidence – and self belief

Confidence comes from hours of practice which help to make skills automatic. Sailors need to be encouraged to use positive self talk, 'I can and I will' not 'I can't do that'. They need to be realistic about their level of ability, and prepared to develop their skills; 'I can't right now, but I am working towards it', not 'I'll never be able to'. Most young sailors have fragile confidence. One way of helping them to protect their confidence is to introduce the Bubble of Self Confidence.

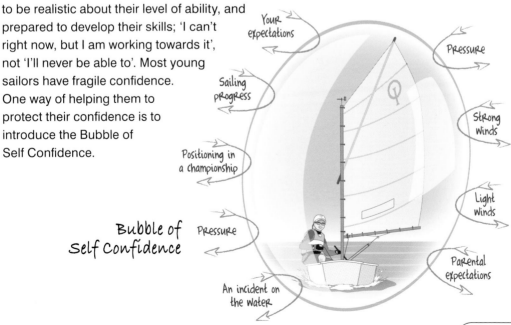

Concentration

There are 3 different types of concentration required of a sailor:

1 – Intense concentration

Concentration required on the start line and after the start.

2 – Sustained concentration

The ability to be aware of the big picture and how it is affecting you around the race course.

3 – Very intense concentration

Concentration needed to hold a lane when sailing upwind, or holding position on the start line.

There are many factors which can affect concentration and it is essential to manage these distractions. One of the best ways is just to focus on the processes.

4 Zones of concentration

When sailing a sailor needs to learn to focus on the different aspects of sailing, and on the right things at the right time. The 4 Zones Model helps sailors to be more selective and divide their attention between the conflicting details they are concentrating on.

1 – Me

Is all about the sailor and how they are feeling while sailing. Are they calm and focused or stressed and anxious? Have they had enough to eat and drink? How are they holding the tiller extension and mainsheet?

2 – Now

Is about what is happening now. Is the rig set up correctly? Is the sailor sailing fast? Are they pointing or footing? Are they over or under sheeted? What about the next wave, the gust the sailor is dealing with, the telltales, or other boats in close proximity? There's a lot going on in the Now Zone.

3 – Next

Is about what's coming next, the next gust, the next group of boats, or the next mark rounding.

4 – Big Picture

Is about remembering that the sailor is in a race and this includes the position of the fleet, tidal stream, wind, effect of headlands or bays, or even clouds moving across the course.

Control – Controlling the controllables

As a coach you need to help sailors focus on things within their control and not worry about factors outside it. For example:

- Boat set up
- How much practice
- Starting priorities
- Tactics
- Food and drink
- Confidence

Get the sailor to list things within their control and then a list of things outside of it. The aim is to get a sailor to focus on what they can control and not worry about things they cannot. Sometimes a sailor will lose control, and this will be exhibited as either anger or anxiety. Simple exercises will help the sailor learn to cope with this. For example:

- Other sailors' results
- Sailing conditions
- Race results

Commitment

Sailing is just one part of a sailor's life and there are many competing distractions. There needs to be a home-school-life-friends-sailing balance. While a sailor is making progress and being successful it is easy to remain committed but as soon as progress stalls, the results don't appear, or the sailor becomes bored or just doesn't enjoy it anymore, the commitment can just ebb away. Having lots of sailing friends can help keep sailors in the sport.

Goal setting can help a sailor get through the tough times, and recognise that it can take a long time to succeed.

Communication

Effective communication is an essential element of mental toughness. Sailors need to learn to communicate well, not to bottle things up and how to talk about issues affecting their performance. This enables them to cope and develop.

Routines

Developing routines is an important element of mental toughness. Routines will help you and your sailors to be organised. The best routines are simple and straightforward, so keep it simple.

Resilience

Resilience is all about coping with pressure and stress. It is also about self belief and the ability to bounce back from disappointment or failure.

Priorities

It is critical to get sailors focusing on priorities. There is no point in a sailor focusing on rig set up while approaching the windward mark on port tack and trying to find a space to get onto the starboard lay line, or thinking about the position of the windward mark while negotiating a set of big waves while sailing upwind.

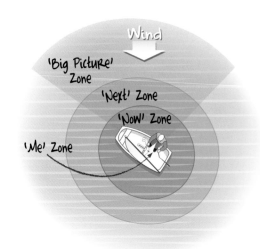

'Sailors need to learn to sail in the here and now.'
Dr Ben Chell, RYA Psychologist

Think correctly under pressure

A valuable technique you can help sailors develop is to Think Correctly Under Pressure, or TCUP. This was developed by Clive Woodward with the England World Cup winning rugby team. Applied to sailing TCUP is about helping sailors to make appropriate decisions when under pressure such as at a start, when crossing other boats or approaching a windward mark.

Pressure

Following on from the idea of TCUP it is important to consider the effect of pressure on a sailor's performance and about how to combat the effects of it in competition.

Pressure can come from the sailor, parents or coach's expectations, fear of failure, sailing conditions or even the competition itself. Sailors need help to manage pressure and those around the sailor need to do what they can to minimise the impact of pressure.

Sailors can be helped to cope with pressure by getting them to focus on the following:

- The 'here and now'.

- Thinking about priorities.

- Countering negative 'I can't' thoughts with positive 'I can' thoughts.

- Constant repetition of drills, routines and games will help a sailor cope under pressure, and appropriate pressure based training will help the sailor develop their own strategies.

- Good boat handling and decision making under pressure is the hallmark of a skilful sailor. However, if pressure is applied too early or inappropriately, skills break down and performance crumbles.

- Sailors must learn to be adaptable to the ever changing dynamics of a race; a lot of practice in many different situations will lead to confidence.

Top tips

✦ Confidence in skills leads to competence.

Competence

This is a model which demonstrates various levels of competence, and is a good way of helping sailors understand their level of knowledge and understanding.

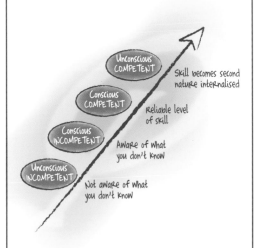

Adapted from WC Howells and others.

Developing independence

Unlike sports where the coach has direct contact during the competition, as soon as a sail boat race starts, the sailor is completely on their own for up to an hour. During that time the sailor has to think about and make their own decisions. Coaches have to make certain that all coaching is channelled towards making the sailor as independent as possible. When achieved then the coach can consider they have been successful.

USE OF CAMCORDERS & VIDEO CLIPS WHEN COACHING

The use of video feedback in the coaching process has become an essential component of coaching. In this section we'll look at the basic use of video cameras when coaching sailing.

Use of video clip feedback

There are 4 key uses for video feedback:

1 – Clips showing good technique

It's useful to have a simple library of clips showing good technique. You can use these at any time to provide great examples of how it should be done.

2 – Feedback for the sailors

Take clips of sailors and use the clips to provide feedback for them.

3 – Analysing coaching

Use the clips to review your coaching and how effective you were at capturing useful clips for yourself to discuss with the sailors.

4 – It's fun

Sailors enjoy looking at video feedback and find it really useful.

Camcorders

There are 4 main types of camcorders or multi use cameras:

1 – Traditional tape camcorders using mini DV tapes.

2 – Hard drive camcorders using a hard drive to save clips.

3 – SD Camcorders, which use SD storage cards to download on to a PC or laptop.

4 – Digital cameras with video recording capability.

Environment

You need to be able to use your camcorder afloat and ashore. Electronics are delicate and some types are available fully waterproof or have housings to prevent water ingress. Be aware of the direction of the sun.

Spray or waves are always a challenge, so keep cleaning the lens. Special anti-droplet liquids are available but I find that licking the lens and drying it with a tissue or a rag works best!

Using the camcorder

Usually the simpler the camcorder the better, and make sure you know how to use it correctly. Attach it to your buoyancy aid with a lanyard (so you don't drop it in the water)! Keep it charged up, it is so frustrating if your camera dies just when you need it – a spare battery is always a good idea.

Types of clips

Technical - detail of technique

For example; tacking, gybing, sheeting, hands, footwork, body movement, accelerating, land drills.

Tactical – involving other boats

For example; starting, mark roundings, boats meeting.

Strategy

Camcorders aren't very useful for coaching strategy. Strategy is too big a subject, unless you can film from a very high position – a bird's eye view.

GPS is now used to help look at strategic considerations, combined with on-line mapping such as Google Earth.

The sun

Be aware of its position when taking clips.

• Away from the sun – sharp crisp clips
• Into the sun – blurring and shadows.

It's easy to take clips when anchored or stationary, the challenge comes when moving!

Filming while driving a coach boat

Most on the water coaching takes place from a small coach boat. On flat water it is a simple and straightforward process to take clips, but in choppy conditions it can be difficult.

Ideally have two people onboard, one driving and one using the camera, but more often than not you will be on your own. Fortunately, Optimists don't travel very fast and are predictable (unlike a Foiling Moth), making it possible to get quite close to the action.

Most coaches will stand up, steer with one hand and use the camera with the other. If you do this, be aware what is going on around you.

When it's really choppy it can be difficult keeping the camera on the sailor. Maybe that's why most Oppy coaches don't win Oscars for best cinematography – just do your best!

Coach boat positioning

The following illustrations will help you to position the coach boat to achieve the best clips in different scenarios.

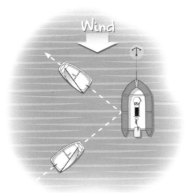

Tacking

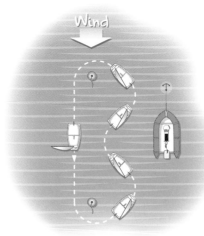

Sailing around a course

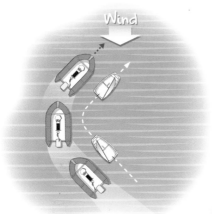

Following a tack

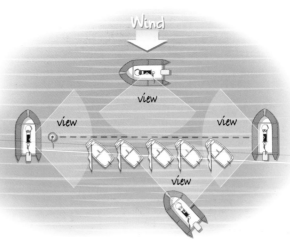

The start

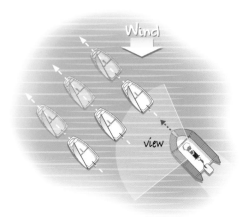

Sailing upwind - from behind

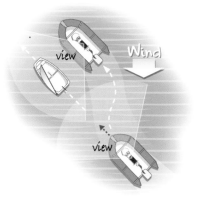

Transition - from behind
to side on

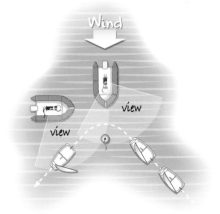

Windward mark rounding -
don't get too close or the wind will
blow you downwind

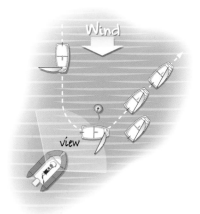

Leeward mark rounding

Sailor feedback

With few exceptions most sailor feedback using video clips will be back on shore.

The key points for a successful feedback session are:

1 – It's good practice to watch a clip at normal speed. Then go back over it using the pause button for discussion and slow motion to give more time to identify what's going on.

2 – Reviewing technical development such as tacking, gybing or speed. You need to have clips of all group members or some sailors will feel left out.

3 – When reviewing tactics, ask sailors to consider their own positions and decisions. This gives multiple outcomes to the review.

Storage and use of clips

There are a number of ways of storing and retrieving clips as camcorders move away from tape to cards. The simplest is to transfer them from your camera to your PC or laptop, putting them into folders for future use. A number of software programmes are available for storing and analysing clips and to post clips onto social networking sites providing wider access, including sites such as Facebook, YouTube or specially designed websites.

Digital stills cameras

These enable you to take a number of pictures in rapid succession, providing a very clear set of sequences – particularly useful in technical skills development, for example tacking and gybing, accelerating.

Top tips

✛ Use a location without distractions.

✛ Be positive and constructive.

✛ Don't focus on the negatives.

✛ Focus on 2–3 well made key points, rather than 10 rushed points.

✛ Be interactive and involve the sailors.

Using GPS sets

Small sets are increasingly used in coaching to track sailors around the race course. The tracks are downloaded into software programmes making it possible to analyse a sailor's performance. This is useful for more advanced Optimist sailors and to look at tacking angles, sailing on lifts and headers, tactics and overall strategy.

 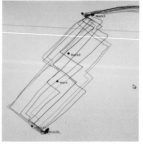

GPS track of sailors' courses

COACH BOATS, SAFETY & TRAINING MARKS

The use of coach boats, general safety and using training marks are key skills for you to learn. This section covers all these essential skills.

Driving a coach boat

Driving a coach boat amongst a group of Optimists takes skill, care and consideration. It's important to remember that sailors may find it intimidating having a coach boat bearing down on them. So when you are in and amongst Optimists drive at a safe speed so you can respond to any Optimists tacking in front of you.

It's essential at all times to wear an engine killcord, and to have the following basic safety equipment;

• Buoyancy aid or lifejacket	• Bucket
• Waterproofs	• Paddle
• Spare killcord	• Fire extinguisher
• First aid kit	• Towline
• VHF radio and mobile phone	• Engine tool kit
• Knife / pliers, screwdriver or multi tool	• Anchor, chain, warp
• Whistle	• Distress flares
• Spares	• Sailor medical information sheet
• Electrical tape or / and duct tape	

Coach boat tips

Preparation

- Have sufficient fuel for the training session and check the oil level.
- Check the boat's painter is shorter than the distance to the propeller. Then if it falls over the side while you are driving, it won't get fouled and cause you embarrassment!
- Check the anchor and warps are long enough.

Driving skills

- Remember that the bows of most coach boats will blow off when stationary downwind – weather cocking.
- Make sure your powerboat handling skills are up to date. RYA Powerboat Handbook G13 makes excellent reading.

Communication afloat

VHF radio

Essential for communication on the sea and inland waters. Waterproof handheld sets are useful and if you attach a lanyard you can clip the VHF to your buoyancy aid.

It is always good practice to have a shore contact when you go afloat.

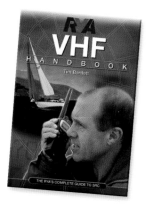
RYA VHF Handbook – G31

VHF radio

Mobile phone

Most coaches have mobile phones. Generally they are not as reliable as VHF and usually not waterproof but useful in an emergency.

Hand held two-way radio

Hand held two-way radios

There are a variety of makes available and they are really handy for communicating with a single sailor during practice racing if you cannot get close to the sailor to help them with decision making or technique.

Getting an Optimist to come alongside you

Coach boat – anchored

When anchored, the sailors simply approach close-hauled then head-up to head-to-wind as you catch them. You can tie the Oppy alongside and the sailors hop out and sit on the side of the coach boat while you have a chat...

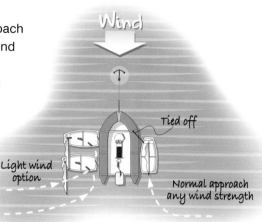

fig. 1

Coach boat – stationary but not anchored

In flat water and little wind an Optimist can easily approach you from many different angles.

But as with any wind and waves, they must approach by sailing at you on a beam-to-close-reach and head-up to stop alongside you.

When a sailor is coming alongside you, your boat needs to be held in a beam reach to close reach position.

fig. 2

Coach boat – coming alongside an Optimist

When approaching a sailor, the sailor needs to stop in a position between a beam reach and a close reach. You then approach on the windward side from behind.

fig. 3

Dealing with a capsize

Capsizing is a natural part of sailing and at some time or another you will be required to provide assistance. Older sailors can usually right and empty their boats, but a younger, lighter or a tired sailor may struggle. As always it's easier to right a boat in flat water rather than waves. Let's take a look at some techniques.

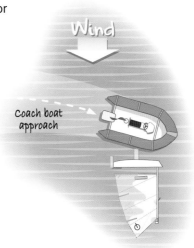

Wind

Coach boat approach

Top tips

+ Always use a killcord when driving a coach boat.
+ Right the capsized Optimist into the wind.
+ Be aware of trailing ropes.
+ Watch out for a sailor in the water.
+ Watch out for other water users.

Recovering a sailor from the water

Should a sailor fall out of their boat or capsize and separate from their boat you will need to pick them up.

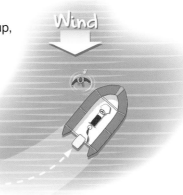

Wind

- Reassure the sailor that you are going to pick them up, and usually approach from downwind.

- Pick up to windward in choppy conditions and from the windward or the leeward side in light winds.

- Once contact is made it is good practice to switch off the engine until the sailor is recovered and in the coach boat.

Towing

Coaches do a lot of towing, and many have their own favourite ways to tow. A very simple way is to tie a loop into the end of each towline and then daisy chain the boats together. You can also tie a loop in the towline close to each boat and connect each boat using a bowline, which is easy for each sailor to untie, or have a clipped towline if you are really keen!

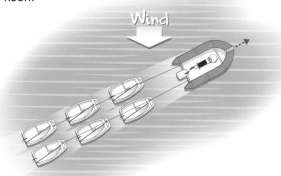

Wind

Top tips

+ Always tow at a safe speed
+ The towline should be easily releasable
+ The sailor should sheet in to prevent the sail from flapping

Breakages

Not many things go wrong with an Optimist, and most can be repaired quickly. The basics you need include a screwdriver, knife, pliers, sail ties, electrical tape, needle, thread and repair sail tape.

Easy things to fix include:

- Replacement sail ties – have a longer sail tie to replace it.

- Tiller fittings coming undone – screwdriver and pliers.

- Mainsheet block shackle pin coming undone – *fig 1*.

- Temporary fix for a broken universal joint – see *fig 2*.

- Sprit block cord snapping – spare cord.

- Loop at head of sail coming undone – sail maker's needle and thread.

fig 1 Preparing a mainsheet spring

fig 2 Temporary repair to a universal joint

Training marks

Training marks to set courses are used and usually include the buoy, a weight to hold it upright, cord and an anchor with chain.

There are various types of buoy including PVC inflatable, round buoys and buoys with poles and flags. Marks can be free floating in deep water or where there is no current. Otherwise the buoy will need to be anchored. I prefer to use the lightest anchor or weight possible because it is easier to haul up after use!

Take care laying or recovering buoys, and make sure the line doesn't get fouled up in your propeller. Streaming the buoy and warp first then lowering the anchor is good practice.

COACHING TECHNIQUES

In this section we will look at some of the everyday coaching techniques you need to use.

Communication

In any sport it is important, and in the noisy world of sail coaching it is even more important that you learn to communicate effectively.

Some key communication skills include:

- Verbal and non-verbal communication
- Listening skills
- Ability to use trigger words
- Provide clear briefings
- Have a high action to talk ratio

- Paraphrase long sentences
- Use diagrams, video and demonstrations
- The use of key words or signals to support activity

Verbal and non-verbal communication

We all communicate verbally and non-verbally. Key points of effective communication include:

- The way you speak, the friendliness, frostiness, enthusiasm, stress or sincerity of your voice.
- The tone and speed of your voice. Try not to speak too quickly. Leave gaps for things to sink in.
- Think about the clothes you are wearing – that slogan on the tee-shirt!
- Remember to remove dark sunglasses – eye contact.

Body language

When coaching you should maintain positive body language. Sailors pick up on negative or disinterested body language very quickly. Remember body language is a two-way process and you need to be able to pick up on how your group is feeling.

Body language includes:

- Eye contact – important but don't overdo it as it can be intimidating!
- Expressions on your face.
- Posture – how you stand or sit.
- Gestures.

There are simple rules of thumb with communication which are worth remembering:

55% of communication is body language

38% of communication is tone of voice

7% of communication is the spoken word

Listening skills

You should listen attentively to your sailors. Try to avoid being distracted. Nodding your head towards a sailor and having eye contact while they are talking is a good way of showing you are really listening.

Why aren't these kids listening?

Trigger Words

Use trigger words or phrases to support your coaching, as they are really useful to help a sailor focus on a key point. Words such as;

ease, squeeze, pause, pounce, smooth, shoulders
steering, pump, head out of boat, focus and smile.

All act as trigger words and aid the learning process.

High action to talk ratio

Whether coaching practical sailing or covering relevant theory, you need to ensure sessions have a high action to talk ratio.

Paraphrasing

Try not to use 20 words when 10 will do. Use shorter sentences making them highly informative.

Feedback

This is essential to the learning process. It can be direct; for example, 'this is what you need to do' which often works well with younger sailors (still developing the basics) and forms part of teaching.

Questions

The use of questions when coaching is a well known and tried technique. If we also provide the answer to a question we deny the student from learning the answer by themselves – quite profound but true.

This all sounds good in theory but in practice, as we are trying to accelerate the learning process, we sometimes have to instruct by subtly providing the answer and using a 'try this', or 'do this' approach. Move on to a more questioning approach when the sailor is more experienced.

Feedback – the RYA Traffic Light Process

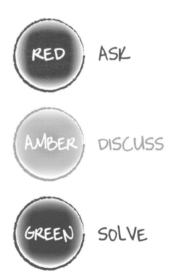

RED — ASK

AMBER — DISCUSS

GREEN — SOLVE

A useful technique which helps provide a structure to giving feedback is to use the RYA Traffic Light Process of ask-discuss-solve.

It is very easy to ask closed questions, and it's OK to ask a closed question such as 'did you enjoy that?' However, you would then need to ask some open questions to continue, such as 'I was really impressed by your start, what do you think helped you get such a good start?' The questions you use can start with the following key words:

Who?, What?, Why?, Which?, When?, Where?, Did?, How?

Fault correction and diagnostic tools

The ability to observe a sailor and analyse what the sailor is doing is an essential coaching skill. A coach needs to have a very good overview of what a good performance looks like. You then need to be selective and prioritise what needs to be worked on in order to help the sailor achieve it. Sometimes it might be just a quick fix; however, mostly it will take much longer to bring about change and improvement.

When observing a manoeuvre such as a tack try using 'STAACCPW' – **Speed, Timing, Accuracy, Adapted, Consistency, Control, Positioning, Weight** help you analyse what is happening.

Speed

How fast or slow, was it passive or dynamic?

Timing

Did they wait until head to wind to roll the boat and how quickly did the sailor cross the boat?

Accuracy

Hand and feet movements.

Adapted

Did the sailor adapt the technique to a gust, lull, flat water or waves?

Consistency

Is the tack consistent each time?

Control

Was the sailor in control throughout the manoeuvre?

Positioning

The position of the sailor in the boat, sat in, perching on the gunwale or hiking.

Weight

How did the sailor use his/her weight to roll the boat?

Measuring and evaluating performance

This is an essential ingredient of successful long term coaching. The following techniques outline how a coach can measure and evaluate a sailor's performance:

Observation

- Using your eyes.
- Video feedback.
- Still pictures.

Analysis

- What, why and when something happened.
- Analysis based on experience.
- Comparison with others.

Evaluation

Usually takes place during and after the activity has taken place. The coach considers the success of the activity and what more needs to be done.

Feedback

This is about providing the sailor with an honest assessment on their performance. It should be positive, constructive, easily understood and helpful to the sailor.

Planning

The final stage and needs to apply what has been learnt to become the goals for future sessions.

Reviewing your own coaching performance

It is important to recognise that as a coach you need to develop as well. You will find it useful to participate in coaches' clinics and workshops and to work alongside other coaches sharing ideas.

One of the most important coach development tools is reflection.

- What went well and why?
- What didn't go so well and why?
- How would you do it differently next time?
- Ask your sailors or other coaches for feedback on your coaching.

THE COACHING PLAN

The most important element behind any successful coach is being well organized and having a plan. Running a coaching session involves leadership and management skills and there are some simple models which will help you to understand your priorities.

Any successful coaching session will include these 4 key elements. Managing them successfully is the key to success.

Coaching kit checklist – Afloat

To run a successful on water coaching session you must have the right equipment to take afloat. An important bit of information you must have when a sailor joins your coaching sessions is to have details of any medical conditions the sailor may have and how to deal with it should anything occur during coaching.

- Watch
- Buoyancy aid or lifejacket
- Waterproofs
- Hat, scarf, gloves (northern winter climates)
- Hat, sunglasses and sun cream (in hot weather)
- Mini whiteboard and pens
- Camera and video camera
- First aid kit
- VHF radio and mobile phone
- Flags or battens for starting

- Knife (Pref. serrated) / multitool
- Wind indicator / compass / anemometer
- Spare engine killcord
- Spares, string, shackles etc.
- Food and drink
- Sailor medical information sheet and medication if required
- Waterproof bag to carry kit
- Training marks
- Notepad and pencil. RYA Wet Notes is ideal.
- Whistle

Coaching kit

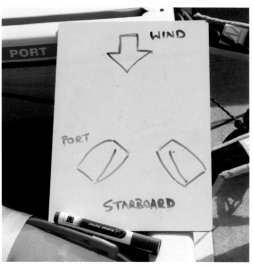

Saves on words!

The coaching process

A simple and yet universal model you can use to run any part of a session is known as **Plan-Prime-Plan-Brief-Do Feedback-Review**. This technique provides you with a useful framework for all of your coaching. Let's look at how it works.

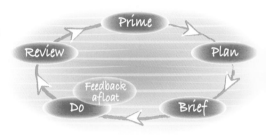

Plan

Before doing anything else you must plan out what you want to achieve and how to do it. You will then be well prepared for the coaching session.

Prime

When working with a group of sailors on a long term basis, it is well worth emailing the group before a particular session takes place. The email should include:

• An outline programme for the coaching session.

• Ask the sailors to start thinking about particular goals and aims for the training.

• Ask the sailors to get a weather and wind forecast / tidal information for the area.

• Get a Google Earth map of the venue and start thinking what the wind might be doing at the venue.

Keep it simple - Have a plan

It is fundamental to have a plan for every session. The following simple plan is a useful tool:

1 – Who are you going to coach?

2 – What level of ability are the sailors?

3 – Where is the location?

4 – Have you worked out a session plan?

5 – How much time do you have to run the session?

6 – Do you have a coach boat, fuel and training marks and maybe a member of crew?

7 – What equipment do you have available?

8 – Think about creating a safe learning environment.

9 – What is the weather forecast, and if you are sailing on coastal waters what is the tide doing?

10 – Have you communicated with the sailors and parents?

11 – Have you organised yourself, your sailing kit, session plan, fed the cat etc?

12 – Will the weather change?

13 – Do you have a simple set of whistle or hand signals?

Briefing

Everyone needs to know the plan, so when briefing your sailors make sure that there are no distractions so everyone understands what's going on. You can confirm understanding by asking the group questions about what they should be doing, although even then they will still come to your coach boat and ask the question 'what are we doing next?'

What to include in the briefing

1 – Use a whiteboard to draw exercises / games or a video to show a specific technique.

2 – Warm up activity.

3 – The main technical session and its aims – no more than 2-3 aims.

4 – Sailors' own personal goals.

5 – Final activity.

6 – Boat set up for the conditions.

7 – Remind group about snacks and drinks.

8 – Sailing area / hazards.

9 – Signals – whistle and hand.

10 – The time to meet on the slipway all ready to go.

11 – Safety.

12 – Timing.

Do and Feedback

When the sailors get on the water you should encourage them to start warming up straight away with some basic warm up games. Following on from the warm up, move on to the main technical exercises making sure that you coach the group as a whole as well as working with individual sailors. Provide the sailors with on the water feedback on their performance.

Remember to use games which are designed to have a learning effect. It is essential to organise games within the context of a sail boat race, whether it is racing, starting, tuning, speed runs etc. There are lots of good games later on in this book.

Communication afloat

It's all very well having great games but you need to be able to communicate them. Here are some tips to help:

• Make sure you can be heard, and seen.

• Face sailors when you talk to them.

• Tie the sailor's boat up alongside your coach boat to avoid distractions.

• Use first names (put names on the back of boats to aid remembering).

• Use eye to eye contact. Try to avoid sunglasses during close communication.

• Be consistent and positive in your approach.

• Use a whistle to attract attention.

• Make sure your sailors can see your face.

Signals

You need to short cut communication afloat. This can be achieved by using hand signals and whistle signals. Some examples of signals are shown below.

2 –

1 –

Go!

You come to me

Follow me

Go home

Classroom coaching kit

Coaching sessions should be fun and as enjoyable as possible. There are a number of basic tools a coach needs to coach successfully:

- Whiteboard, pens or a chalkboard and chalk
- TV screen or digital projector
- Flip chart

- Magnetic boats to use on magnetic white board (RYA Code MBP)
- Books and DVDs
- Video clips
- Racing Rules of Sailing (RYA Code YR1)

Review

When back ashore it's time to review the session and draw out the learning points. If it's been a very physical training session you should consider getting sailors to do a warm down and gentle stretches. There is a temptation to do a brain dump and talk about everything you saw – avoid this and stick to key points. Remember the Memory Game. Use video clips, whiteboards or magnetic boats to make the review interesting.

Don't do most of the talking. It was the sailors' experience and they need to talk about it. Your role is to help the sailors draw out the lessons. It's also good practice to get the sailors to complete their sailing diaries.

Remote coaching – feedback

After the coaching session has finished email the sailors and get them to reflect on the session. With younger sailors it's good practice getting parents involved in reflecting on a coaching session.

- Keep the feedback simple, making sure it is positive. Praise efforts not just results.

- Send words, pictures or diagrams to reinforce key points.

- Send a video or photos with questions.

- Quizzes.

Self coaching

One of the most important aspects of good coaching is to get sailors to become their own coach. They have to learn to analyse their own performance and start taking control of their training. Sailors should be encouraged to do their own training in a safe environment, learn how to talk to each other and provide each other with positive feedback.

A simple process for the sailor to use is Plan-Do-Review (see *fig 1* page 66). The sailor plans the activity, does it and then reflects on the outcome.

Coach-sailor partnership

The key to helping sailors achieve their potential is to make sure that there is an effective coach-sailor partnership. The following will help you to develop a winning strategy:

- The coach and sailor should establish the culture and ground rules for the sessions.

- The programme and goals need to be agreed by the coach, sailors and parents.

- You must know each sailor's preferred learning style.

- You need to understand how to help the sailor to learn.

- You should make sure that there is good communication.

- You need to provide great opportunities for the sailor to learn.

- Feedback needs to be a two-way process.

- Have no favourites, treat everyone equally.

CREATING THE EXERCISES, ROUTINES & GAMES

A creative aspect of a coach's role is to select and develop exercises which go into any coaching session. When coaching less experienced sailors you will be setting the activities. However as sailors become more experienced they should be involved in selecting and developing their exercises. Remember to think about Teaching Games for Understanding and the RYA Skills Model when creating activity sessions.

Activity sessions

- It is useful to have a theme for each activity session.
- Games should be fun.
- Remember that games have multiple outcomes, and some you may not even have considered.
- It is important to have progressions within exercises, routines and games.
- The activity needs to be appropriate for the weather conditions and the sailor's ability.

- Keep the sailor active on the water.
- The session should simulate real situations on the race course.
- There should be some time for the sailor to practise without you actively coaching.
- Allow some time for sailor feedback and reflection when on the water.
- The activity needs to be safe.

Designing games

Start by thinking about what you want to achieve from the session, and use exercises and games which have a direct relevance to the race course. Games you will develop will usually include:

- Technique
- Tactics
- Fun
- Rules and strategy
- Physical and emotional development
- Opportunities to learn

Involve the sailor

With the exception of basic level sailors, it is possible to include sailors in the choice of exercises and games to play to achieve selected outcomes. It is important to have a particular focus within any exercise or game, and necessary to recognise that each sailor may have their own particular goals within the activity which need to be addressed. As a result many exercises will have multiple outcomes.

Delivering exercises and games

There are lots of ways of delivering exercises and games and here is a simple way to get started.

- Explain the rules and talk through the game. What is its aim?

- Walk through the game with the sailors.

- Include on the water feedback.

- Review the game.

Consider how long a game should last and end it just as the sailors peak in performance and before they become disinterested. Sailors will lose interest in the best game if it is overused.

There are many games you can use later on in this book. Don't be afraid of creating your own.

SETTING UP THE BOAT

As soon as possible Oppy sailors need to learn to rig their own boats. They will then take ownership of their boat rather than see it as something Mum, Dad or the coach does for them!

Of course younger sailors will require help and support, but older sailors should actively want to rig their own boats.

There are plenty of rigging games to play, featuring learning to rig the boat, naming the parts of the boat and rig and how to tie sail ties for light, medium and strong wind conditions.

Make it interesting and sailors will listen!

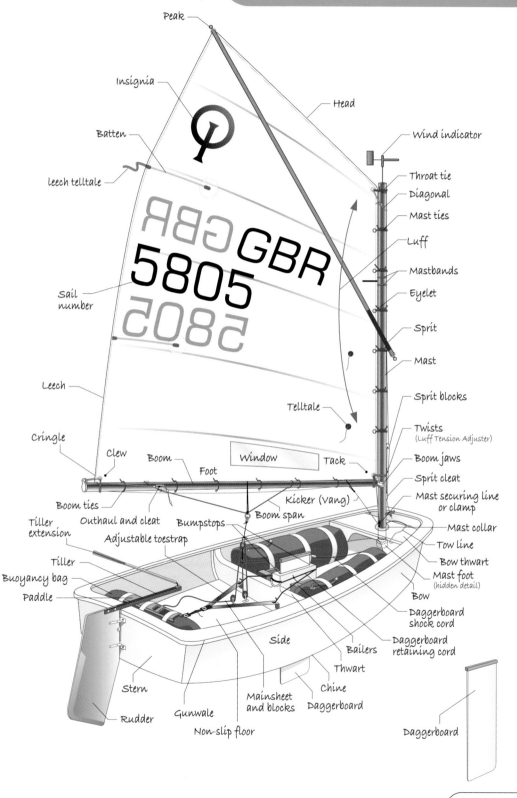

Peak

Insignia

Batten

leech telltale

Sail number

Leech

Cringle

Clew

Boom

Boom ties

Tiller extension

Outhaul and cleat

Adjustable toestrap

Bumpstops

Boom span

Tiller

Buoyancy bag

Paddle

Stern

Rudder

Gunwale

Non-slip floor

Mainsheet and blocks

Side

Bailers

Thwart

Chine

Daggerboard

Foot

Window

Tack

Kicker (Vang)

Head

Wind indicator

Throat tie

Diagonal

Mast ties

Luff

Mastbands

Eyelet

Sprit

Mast

Sprit blocks

Telltale

Twists
(Luff Tension Adjuster)

Boom jaws

Sprit cleat

Mast securing line or clamp

Mast collar

Tow line

Bow thwart

Mast foot
(hidden detail)

Bow

Daggerboard shock cord

Daggerboard retaining cord

Daggerboard

GBR 5805

Equipment

The Optimist is an interesting boat. It's a one-design boat but there are many suppliers of hulls, rigs, foils and sails. There is always the latest big thing and plenty of rumours about what is fast. Coaches are continually asked for advice about what to buy. Contrary to popular belief there is no great mystery.

Hulls – Most hulls are very similar, but check they are scratch free and have a non-slip coating on the bottom of the boat – there is nothing worse than a sailor losing confidence by falling over all the time.

Toestraps – should be adjusted for the leg length of the sailor.

Toestraps

- Small sailors need toestraps which are longer or moved further outboard.

- Taller sailors need to hike off both toestraps to ensure that their knees remain inside the gunwale.

Masts – are surprisingly similar in stiffness. Check the friction collar (if fitted) is level with the bow thwart.

Booms – Bendy booms distort sail shape and should be avoided. 45mm booms have a good blend of stiffness with a little bit of flexibility.

Sprits – Bendy sprits don't help the leech stand firm, so generally stiffer sprits are best.

Foils – There is always a great interest in foils, should they be stiff, flexible or twist? For most sailors a regular daggerboard and rudder will be fine. There can be some advantage in heavier sailors using a stiffer board. Foils with fine entries (leading edge profile) go well on flat water and those with more rounded entries are more forgiving when sailing on the sea.

Sails

Always the hot topic of conversation around the dinghy park. There are 3 basic types:

1 – Cross cuts

2 – Radials

3 – Hybrid (a cross between a cross cut and a radial).

Generally they come in flat, medium and heavy cuts, for different weights of sailors.

All three designs work well. The cross cut is probably the most forgiving and needs least adjustment; the other two need more adjustment to get the best out of them. Radial sails have their shape locked in, whereas it is possible to adjust the shape of a cross cut more easily. Some sailors say that they can read a cross cut more easily than a radial.

Setting up sails

Luff – Usually soft in light winds, medium in medium winds and firm in strong winds. Make sure you read the sail maker's tuning guide because all sails are set up differently.

Outhaul – Mostly flatter in light and strong winds, fuller in medium winds, and fuller in choppy conditions to provide more power.

Sprit – Crease at the throat to open up the leech in light and strong winds and no crease in medium winds.

Kicker (Vang) – Only enough to stop the boom rising too much downwind in light conditions and progressively tighter until very tight in windy conditions. It is a good idea to get the sailors to learn to adjust their own kickers (vangs) while afloat.

Kicker (Vang)

Mainsheet and its attachment

Mainsheets need to be comfortable to hold. Some sailors prefer thin or tapered mainsheets and some sailors prefer thicker mainsheets. Some sailors prefer a 3:1 mainsheet and some prefer a 4:1 using a double mainsheet block. It's all down to personal preference.

Bigger sailors prefer to have the mainsheet attachment on the boom further forward so that it is easier to cross the boat when tacking or gybing.

Mainsheet showing 3:1 purchase

Mainsheet showing double block and 4:1 purchase

Tuning Guide

Most sail makers produce tuning guides for their sails, which vary slightly in the optimum amount of luff tension, outhaul and sprit tension required. The following tuning guide acts as a good starting point for an Optimist.

Wind Strength	Upwind Light Force 1-2	Upwind Medium Force 2-4	Upwind Strong Force 4-6+	Reach Light Force 1-2
Mast Rake	Basic setting 282-284cms (111-112 inches) measured without kicker from the top of the mast to the top of rear gunwale.			◀·····
Mast Ties	Top and bottom eased to 6-7mm middle 2-3mm off touching mast or, if lazy, all ties about 5mm off mast.	All ties 4-5mm off mast. It's personal choice.	All ties 3-4mm off mast, for heavier sailors top and bottom ties just off mast, middle ties 4-5mm off mast.	◀·····
Boom Ties	5mm at the ends and up to 7-8mm in the middle.			
Kicker (Vang)	Slack.	Just loose upwind and getting tighter.	Tight becoming very tight.	Slack.
Outhaul	Slightly tighter than smooth foot shape.	Smooth foot shape.	Firm, but not too tight because you still need power in bottom of sail.	◀·····
Luff	Slack, to keep draft back allowing pointing.	Slack to medium as wind increases, to pull draft forward. If choppy, firmer to give more power but less pointing.	Tighter, to pull draft forward and open leech.	◀····
Sprit	Crease at throat.	Throat creases just disappear.	Tight, lightweights ease sprit to show crease at throat depowering the sail. When very windy all have an eased sprit.	◀····

Reach Medium Force 2-4	Reach Strong Force 4-6+	Run Light Force 1-2	Run Medium Force 2-4	Run Strong Force 4-6+
• • • • ▶				
	Radial sails might need the mast slightly further forward than cross cut sails.			
• • • • •				
	Make sure ties don't stretch.			
As upwind. Lightweights tight.	Very tight.	Slack.	As upwind. Lightweights tight.	Very tight or you won't get downwind.
• • • • ▶	All sails have different foot lengths so you must adjust your sail accordingly. Mark the settings on your boom.			
• • • • • •				
	All sails are designed differently. Some like a generally softer luff tension and others firmer tension. Check your sail tuning guide. Set luff tension using twists on the boom and the pin stop on the mast. The diagonal tie setting is really, really important and make sure you replace the diagonal if it starts to wear.			
• • • • • •				

Tuning Guide

Wind Strength	Upwind Light Force 1-2	Upwind Medium Force 2-4	Upwind Strong Force 4-6+	Reach Light Force 1-2
Mainsheet & Boom Span	2:1 or 3:1. Maybe use lightweight 6mm sheet.	3:1 purchase, 7-8mm non absorbent mainsheet.	3:1 or 4:1 purchase, 7-8mm non absorbent mainsheet.	◀ · · · ·
Sheeting	Boom just outside corner of boat. Keep leech telltales flowing.	Sheet into corner, ease in lulls. Keep leech telltales flowing.	Sheeted into corner, ease in gusts.	Keep telltales flowing.
Daggerboard (Mark positions on the board)	Down.	Down. (Lightweights can raise the board if a little overpowered.)	Up to 100mm up, even for heavier sailors, if struggling to hold boat upright.	½ way up.
Light Weight Sailing Position	Progressively kneel by mainsheet block, sit on thwart then perch on side, bottom in shoulders out.	Sit on side, bottom in, shoulders out. Shoulders slightly back to lift bow over chop.	Hike heaps, dynamic body movement, shoulders to back of boat to get over each wave.	Sit on thwart, then perch on side.
Heavy Weight Sailing Position	Kneel between mainsheet or sit on thwart. Bottom in, shoulders out.	Perch on side, bottom in, shoulders out. Start shoulders back to lift bow over chop.	Hike dynamically, weight back to get through waves.	Sit on thwart, then perch on side.
Steering	Smooth, use body weight to steer. Little use of rudder.	Smooth, still using body weight to steer. Gradually use rudder a little to get through chop.	Use more rudder to sail through chop and waves.	Smooth, use body to steer.

Reach Medium Force 2-4	Reach Strong Force 4-6+	Run Light Force 1-2	Run Medium Force 2-4	Run Strong Force 4-6+
Generally the boom span wants to be tight, so set the depth to about 80mm. Use a mainsheet strop of up to 225mm (11 inches) between the bottom and top mainsheet blocks to reduce the amount of mainsheet you use and reduce windage. Bigger sailors can move the mainsheet position on the boom strop forward to nearly above the thwart to give more room to tack without sinking the back of the boat.				
Keep telltales flowing.	Keep telltales flowing.	Boom out to 90/95°.	Boom out to 90°.	Boom out to about 80°.
½ way up.	¾ way up.	Tip just showing or pulled right up.	¾ way up.	¾ way up.
Hike, shoulders slightly back.	Hike heaps, slide forward to trim boat when planing.	Kite.	Kiting.	Keep boat fairly flat.
Hike, shoulders slightly back.	Hike heaps, slide forward to trim boat when planing.	Almost fully kited.	Fully kited.	Slightly kited / keep boat flat when windy.
Smooth – using body to steer. Bear away in gusts, head up in lulls.	Use little more rudder, bear away in gusts, head up in lulls.	Smooth, use body to steer.	Smooth, use body to steer.	Use more rudder to sail through chop and catch waves. Have fun!

Leech

Leech shape is all important in an Optimist, and it takes time for the sailor to get the shape right. The combined effect of mainsheet tension, sprit and kicker will significantly affect the shape of the leech. Generally open leeches are needed for light and strong winds, and a more closed leech is needed for medium winds sailing on flat water.

Adjusting the rig on the water

Light wind set up, leech open and crease at the throat

Medium wind set up, no crease at throat, firm leech

Strong wind set up, sail flatter and leech twisted off

Measurement

The Optimist is a one design boat strictly controlled by a wide range of measurements. If you are taking sailors to competitions make sure that they have a valid measurement and buoyancy certificate.

Other Stuff

Don't forget bailers, paddle, protest flag, spare sail ties, food, drink etc.

Land drills are great for learning and group discussion

COACHING BASIC BOAT HANDLING

Correctly coaching the basics of sailing is the most important foundation for a young sailor's future success. If young sailors are coached well from the beginning they will learn the mechanics of movement in a boat which will become second nature and lead to rapid progress. Young sailors who start off crawling across the boat on their knees often find it difficult to unlearn poor technique which holds up their learning process later on.

Now we will take a look at coaching basic skills.

Wind awareness

Developing a sailor's wind awareness is essential, and in the early stages it is very important to keep referring to the wind direction until it becomes second nature. The following points of sailing will help sailors understand how wind direction affects their boat. When out on the water it is always useful to refer to the wind direction.

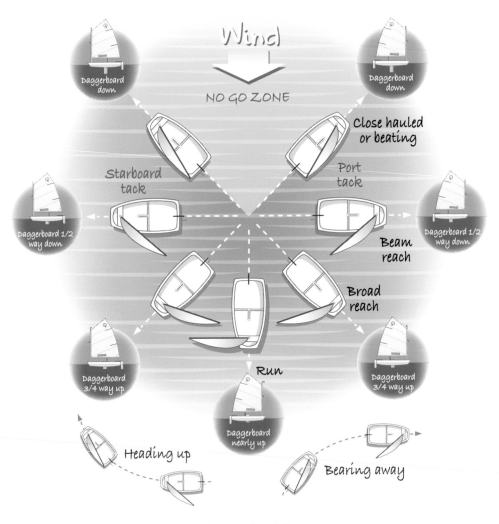

Points of sailing

Land drills

These play an exceptionally important role in developing a sailor's skills. You can use them to develop the basic movements across and around the boat. We'll take a look at some land drill options to use to develop sailors' basic routines.

The basic routines you can develop using land drills include:

- Sheet in, sheet out (start and stop)
- Tacking
- Gybing
- Running
- Body position in the boat
- Adjusting the sprit and kicker (vang)

Top tips

+ Use simple language.
+ Use key words to follow the actions.
+ Praise success and support the sailor through difficulty.
+ Many manoeuvres have three phases, Entry – Mid phase – Exit.

Land drills develop technique

Coach working with a group of young sailors

Boat handling on the water

The following sequence provides examples of boat handling on the water.

Tacking

1 This sailor starts from sitting in, heads up to head to wind

Knees forward

2 Sailor sits on the side and rolls the boat to windward pushing the tiller away

3 Sailor ducks under the boom

Hold end of extension

4 Sailor hops across with mainsheet hand on daggerboard keeping weight low and leaning forward

5 Look forward, shoulders forward, swap hands

6 Sail away

Gybing

1 Sailing on a run, daggerboard down

2 Lean in and grab falls of mainsheet

3 Steer and pull boom over head

4 Hop or step across the boat

5 Either swap hands and / or sit down and swap hands

6 Sail away

Reaching

1 Light wind reach, don't forget to ease the sprit

2 Fast reach, main trimmed perfectly, leeward telltales horizontal

Run

1 Kiting down a run, boat heeled over on top of the sailor

2 Fast run in waves

The Five Essentials of Sailing

Most of the basic on the water exercises can be related back to the 5 Essentials of Sailing, which were developed by Bob Bond, a GBR sailing coach in the 1970s, and are still in use today. Let's take a look at them and you can then refer to them when you are coaching.

Sail setting

Making sure the sailor sets the sail correctly, from at beginner level by sheeting in until the sail just stops flapping, to using telltales at a more advanced level.

Balance (heel)

Sailing the boat upright or deliberately heeling it to windward or leeward.

Trim

The fore and aft trim of the boat.

Daggerboard

Making certain that the daggerboard is in the correct position for each point of sailing.

Course sailed

Sailing efficiently upwind and getting around the race track.

A well set up boat helps produce results!

Basic sailing exercises

Sailors must learn to be able to control their boats, often in very confined spaces. These games and endless variations are great in developing basic sailing skills.

Reach tack reach and reach gybe reach are basic skills. The aim is to make sure that the sailor is confident and feels safe whilst taking these early steps afloat.

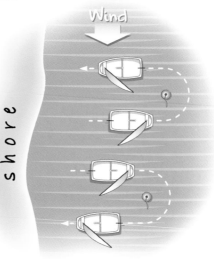

Hovering next to a buoy

Slowing down and stopping

Slowing down or speeding up

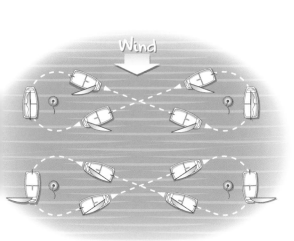

Figure of 8 tacking and gybing

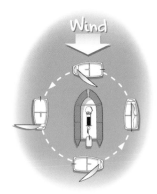

Circle the coach boat

The Woodhead warm up

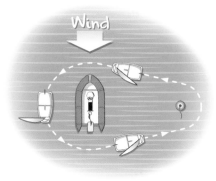

Circle the coach boat variation

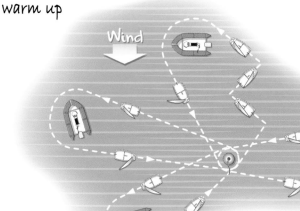

This game was developed by coach Dave Woodhead and involves a fixed training mark and moving the coach boat to different positions.

Follow the leader head up and bear away

Follow the leader, tack off or gybe off and go to the back

This game gives everybody the opportunity to lead. You are also able to observe them at close quarters.

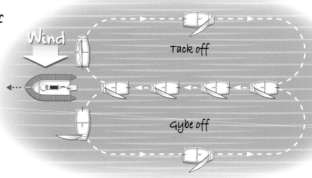

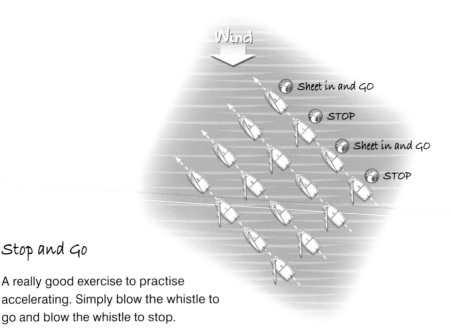

Stop and Go

A really good exercise to practise accelerating. Simply blow the whistle to go and blow the whistle to stop.

A variety of ways to sail upwind

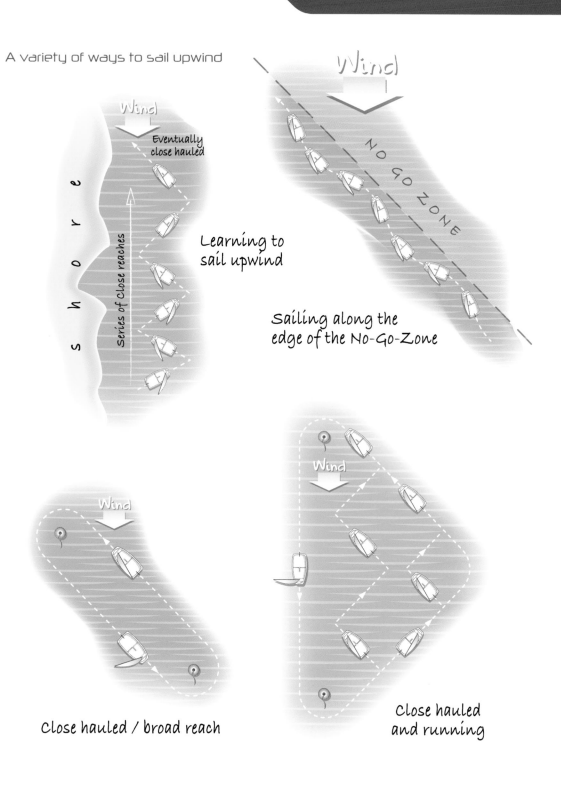

Wind

Eventually close hauled

shore

Series of close reaches

Learning to sail upwind

Wind

NO GO ZONE

Sailing along the edge of the No-Go-Zone

Wind

Close hauled / broad reach

Wind

Close hauled and running

Tacking on the whistle

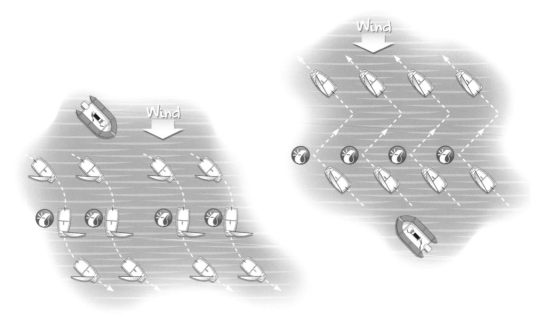

Gybing on the whistle

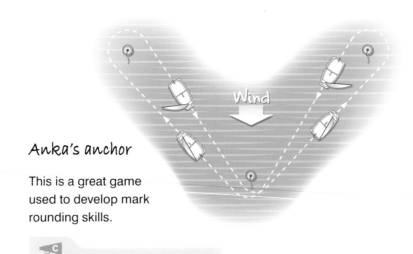

Anka's anchor

This is a great game used to develop mark rounding skills.

Anka, a former Polish Optimist coach, really likes this game.

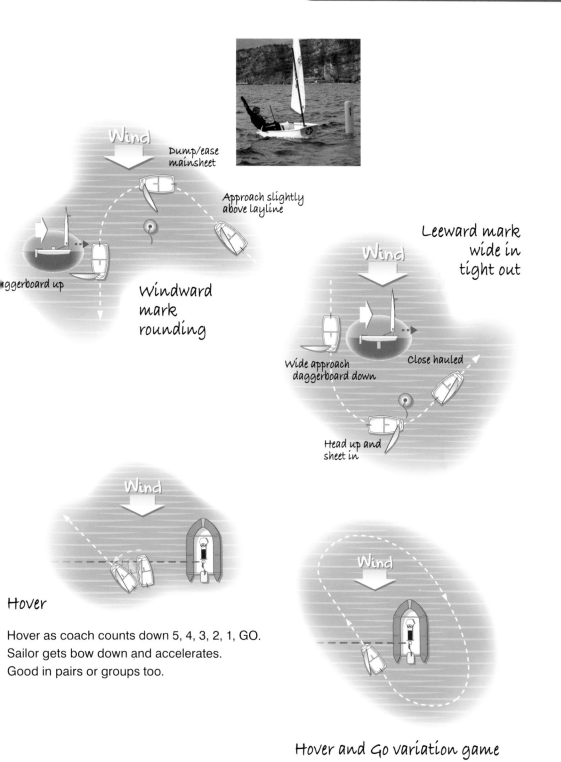

Wind

Dump/ease mainsheet

Approach slightly above layline

ggerboard up

Windward mark rounding

Leeward mark wide in tight out

Wind

Wide approach daggerboard down

Close hauled

Head up and sheet in

Wind

Hover

Hover as coach counts down 5, 4, 3, 2, 1, GO.
Sailor gets bow down and accelerates.
Good in pairs or groups too.

Wind

Hover and Go variation game

Heel

Heel has a significant effect on an Optimist. Heeling a boat to windward will help it bear away and heeling it to leeward will help it head up. Practising heeling a boat to help it steer will help with more advanced sailing skills later on.

Heeling to leeward to help the boat spin upwards close hauled

Fun games

All the exercises and games you use should be fun and along with more formal games there are lots of fun games to play to develop skills. Include the following and I am sure you will think of many more.

Corks and Balls

Lay a square using 4 buoys – all the sailors have to stay within the square. Throw loads of balls or corks in the water and get the sailors to sail around picking them out of the water.

Good for – boat handling Rules – no collisions

Sponge Tag

Using buoys lay a perimeter. One boat is tag and has to throw a sponge into another boat so it is tagged. Play with one sponge or multiple sponges.

Good for – boat handling Rules – no collisions

Balloons

Lay a perimeter using buoys and tie a balloon on a string to the transom of each boat. The aim is to pop the opposition's balloons.

Good for – boat handling Rules – no collisions

Sprit Race

If no wind, take the sprits off and row around a course.

Pumping, rocking, rolling and sculling race

In no wind sailors get around the course using these illegal techniques.
They quickly learn what is legal and not legal under Racing Rule 42.

Rigging Race

Sailors rig then get scored out of 10 for the various elements.

Capsize Recovery Race

Sailors capsize one at a time and then are timed up to bailing out their boats.

5 Essentials Wrong Game

Sailors sail around a course using the 5 Essentials of Sailing incorrectly on each leg of the course. A funny game and drives home the need to get the 5 Essentials right.

Simon Says

Sailors sail around the course doing Simon says, stop, start, stand up, sit down, stand up do a pirouette, stand up, tack, stand up, gybe etc etc.

Musical Buoys

Set up a start line with a short windward leg. The sailors sail round the two buoys either in a figure of eight or a sausage, then when the whistle goes the sailors sail up around the windward mark and back through the line to finish. You can vary the bias and soon the sailors start working out the best position to get to the windward mark first. Good also as a shore drill.

Catch up Games

A competitive automatic skills game with a tactical element. Lay any course you like – sausage, triangle, square, diamond course etc. One sailor or a group starts at one buoy and the other sailor / group at another buoy. The game stops each time one catches the other, scores a point and starts again.

Shore based Start Line

On land set up a start line and get the sailors to work out bias, get transits and practise starting.

There are many other games you can play but be creative and make sure they have a purpose and simple rules.

ADVANCED BOAT HANDLING & SPEED

In this section we discuss how to help you to develop sailors' advanced boat handling skills. The aim is to teach sailors to have very good automatic boat handling skills which stand up under the pressure of competition.

As sailors become more experienced there is a temptation for them to think there is no need to keep working on the basics. But, just like with good footballers or hockey players, there is a real need to keep working on the fundamentals. The real challenge as a coach is to produce creative exercises and games which enable sailors to practise without feeling bored or de-motivated.

Slow speed boat handling skills are so important at a more advanced level; many of the following exercises will help your sailors develop excellent and confident slow speed boat handling.

Posture and hiking technique

All sailors need good posture and there are 3 main principles to follow which should ensure that Optimist sailors don't injure themselves sailing.

Neutral Spine and Sit up Tall

Spines have natural curves (1). We need to find a sailor's neutral spine position as this will minimize risk of injury. The aim is to find the mid point between slumping forward...

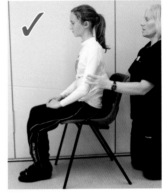

1 Sit up tall

(2) ...and the sailor arching their back too much – the bumble bee back.

2 Bumble bee back

Knee alignment

Good knee alignment is essential for sailors (3). Knees should be in line with the shoulders and feet should be neutral – not pointing in or out too much when walking. Knees must not be forward of toes when positioned standing.

3 Good knee alignment and shoulders

Do the V Sit

One good way to develop good posture is to develop the V sit – (1). Get sailors to help each other practise this position. They will learn quicker!

1 Sit up tall, arms crossed hold for 15 seconds and rest, then repeat

Hiking technique

Good hiking technique is essential to prevent injury and because young sailors are growing it is essential to make sure that the toestraps are adjusted correctly. When sailors become taller they might need to hike using both toestraps.

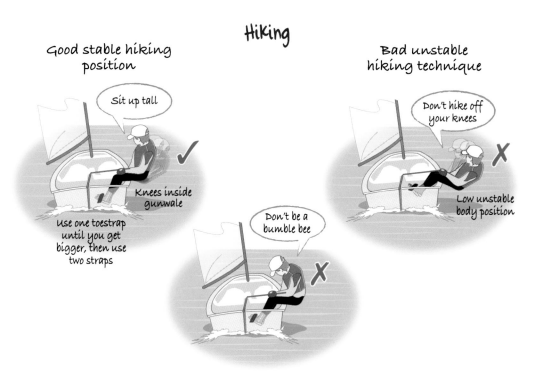

Hiking

Good stable hiking position

Sit up tall

Knees inside gunwale

Use one toestrap until you get bigger, then use two straps

Don't be a bumble bee

Bad unstable hiking technique

Don't hike off your knees

Low unstable body position

Advanced boat handling games

The next set of games are designed to develop advanced boat handling. Remember, you can use these games in light, medium or strong winds and in flat or choppy water. Be careful because if you overdo even the best exercises, sailors will become bored with them, so make sure you build progressions and variety into your games.

Tacking

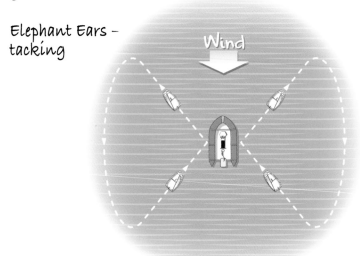

Elephant Ears –
tacking

1 – Start close hauled

2 – Lean in / squeeze the mainsheet

3 – Steer to head to wind

4 – Roll the boat at head to wind, pulling up through front foot under toestrap

5 – Knees forward

6 – Feet underneath

7 – Cross boat using step, hop or strap to strap tack

8 – Straighten rudder, grab gunwale

9 – Roll the boat flat, shoulders forward, lean forward

10 – Squeeze the mainsheet

11 – Swap hands

12 – Carry on.

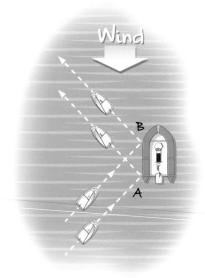

Elephant Ears
variations

Stages of a tack

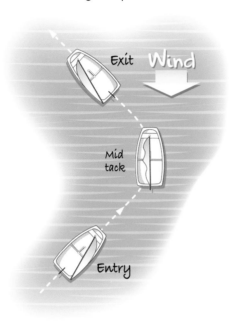

Exit Wind

Mid tack

Entry

Gybing

Gybing process:

1 – Start sailing on a broad reach

2 – Sheet in a little

3 – Steer gently into the gybe

4 – Lean in and grab the falls of the mainsheet

5 – Pull the sail over your head, keeping the rudder straight

6 – Leading with the tiller extension, step lightly across the boat, leading with the back foot

7 – Sit down and swap hands.

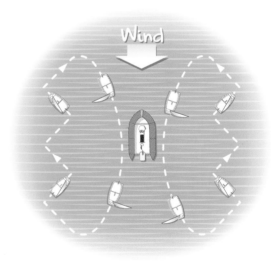

Wind

Elephant Ears – gybing

Half tack

Practising the half tack is a good way for sailors to get used to the point of maximum heel then rolling the boat flat.

Tacking No Hands Game

A simple and fun game to play. The sailor starts going upwind and then lets go of the tiller extension and repeatedly tacks. This develops good body movement and self awareness. Start off in lighter winds!

1 Let go of the tiller extension

2 Tack and cross boat

4 Then tack again

3 Boat comes up head to wind

5 Duck under boom and carry on

Catch Up Game

The aim of this game is to play catch up. When one member of one team catches the other team, stop the game. The winning team scores one point and then the game starts again.

A great boat handling and tactical awareness game.

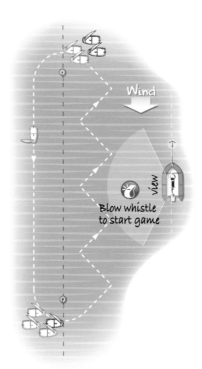

Wind

Blow whistle to start game

view

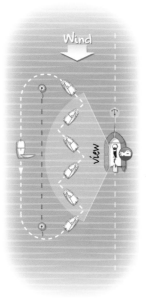

Wind

view

Corridor Game

A simple game which makes the sailors sail up a narrow corridor and the coach can then coach the sailors.

Gutbuster and variations

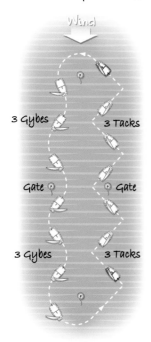

Wind

3 Gybes   3 Tacks

Gate   Gate

3 Gybes   3 Tacks

Wind

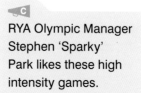

RYA Olympic Manager Stephen 'Sparky' Park likes these high intensity games.

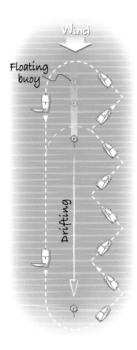

Wind

Floating buoy

Drifting

Creeping Death

Graham Vials, a well known Optimist and 420 coach, recommends this game as it creates pressure.

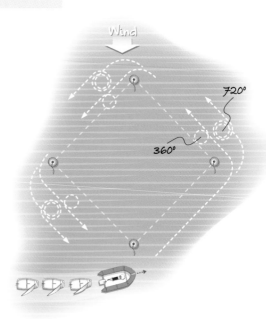

Wind

720°

360°

720° 360° Game

- The first boat to a mark scores 2 points and does a 720°

- The second boat to a mark scores 1 point and does a 360°

- The first boat to 7 points wins the game

- Another variation is to sail around the course and create a gap one boat length ahead of another boat, do a 360° and score a point.

Wind

Bear away
Run

Tack

Close hauled

Tack etc

START

Gybe

Head up
Close hauled

Whistle Game

Each time the whistle blows follow the routine in the illustration.

Wind

Sprit OFF

Sprit On Sprit Off Game

Sprit ON

In light and medium winds ease the sprit after rounding the windward mark

In light winds it's possible to lean forward and put the sprit on again. Alternatively, after rounding the mark ease the mainsheet, stand, step forward, sprit back on and carry on

360°s or 720°s Game

Learning to do a 360° or a 720° well is essential in sailing. They need to be carried out as a penalty for a Rule 2 infringement, Rule 42 infringement or for touching a mark.

Key points for a 720° turn:

1 – Bear away, lean out, ease the mainsheet and use lots of rudder

2 – As the boat gybes let go of the tiller extension

3 – Cross the boat sheeting in hard

4 – The boat will spin itself into a tack

5 – Tack, lean out, ease the mainsheet and bear away

6 – As the boat gybes let go of the tiller extension

7 – Cross the boat sheeting in hard

8 – The boat will spin itself into the next tack

9 – Grab the tiller extension while tacking, bear away to close hauled and carry on.

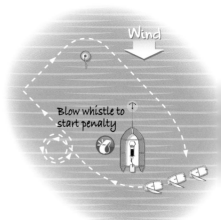

The situation a sailor finds themselves in will dictate starting with a tack or bearing away into a gybe. For example, if they are sailing close hauled without any boats around them they should tack first. Similarly if they were on a run they should gybe first.

A great time to complete a 720° turn in is between 11-14 seconds.

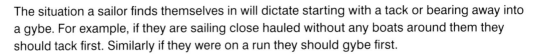

Steering and upwind speed

There is no doubt that excellent speed, accurate steering and good mainsheet management upwind are essential components of good upwind sailing technique. Sailors should continually practise steering to become skilful, always remembering that it is much harder to steer well in shifty conditions than in stable winds.

The basics:

1 – Change gear by anticipating what will happen next.

2 – Use of telltales and wind indicator.

3 – Smooth sailing.

4 – Head out of the boat, now and next zones.

5 – Try to keep a constant angle of heel.

6 – Minimal rudder movement.

7 – Squeeze the main in gusts and ease the main in the lulls.

8 – Move body weight out in gusts and back in lulls.

9 – Adjust sprit tension in lulls and gusts.

Sailing upwind in waves

Sailing an Optimist in waves requires good technique and skill. These are the key elements to successful sailing upwind in waves.

1 – Keeping the boat moving as fast as possible.

2 – Point up over the waves and bearing away down the back of the waves.

3 – Lean back as the boat goes up the wave and upright or slightly forward down the back of the wave.

4 – Keep the boat dry (don't forget to bail).

5 – Keep as much of the boat as possible in the water.

6 – **A longer waterline = a faster boat.**

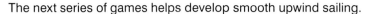

The next series of games helps develop smooth upwind sailing.

Mast Rake Game – A great game to develop feel

• Half the group rake their masts far forward.

• Half the group rake their masts well back.

• In pairs, the sailors compare and contrast how their boats are sailing upwind.

• Sailors swap boats to experience the opposite effects.

• Next, sailors (in pairs) complete a number of upwind tuning runs adjusting their mast rakes until it feels about right.

• When ashore check out the mast rakes with a tape measure and discuss.

Blindfold Game

- A great game for developing feel and communication.
- One sailor is sighted.
- One sailor is blindfolded.
- The sighted sailor guides the blindfolded sailor around the course.

Blindfold upwind

- Play the game in a safe place.
- Each sailor comes alongside the coach boat.
- The sailor sails off upwind and puts the blindfold on.
- Sailor then sails upwind for 2-3 minutes.

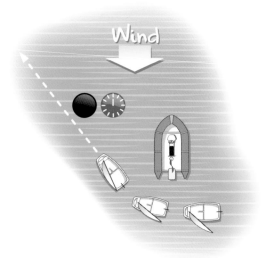

Tethered Rudders Game

The game minimises the use of the rudder and encourages the use of body weight and mainsheet to steer the boat.

Tether the tiller to the toestrap using shockcord, allowing a small amount of movement

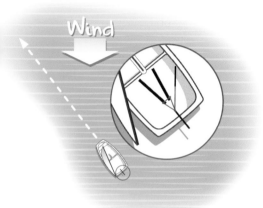

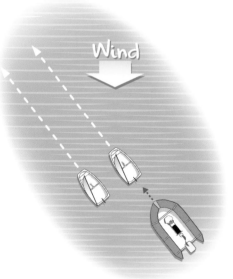

Steering Game

Following on from tethered tillers this game encourages smooth sailing upwind, micro management of the mainsheet and their new found skills.

Telltales – upwind Game

Take off the wind indicator and get the sailors to use their telltales to sail upwind. Sailors look at the differing effects on the telltales:

1 – The effect the sprit has on telltales close to the sprit.

2 – Telltales which catch on seams.

3 – The best length for telltales, and what they are made of.

4 – What happens to the telltales when pointing or footing.

5 – The leeward telltale should always be horizontal.

6 – The windward telltale should be horizontal but the mast and sprit often cause the windward telltale to spin and dance around.

7 – The leech telltales should be flowing 70-80% of the time.

Sailing upwind using the telltales

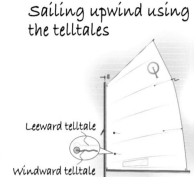

Leeward telltale

Windward telltale

Wind

Pointing

Footing

Keelboat Game

Develops awareness of heel and mainsheet tension:

1 – Sailors sit on the bottom on the wrong side of the boat.

2 – Then sail or race around a course adjusting the mainsheet to keep the boat upright.

> **c**
> NZL coach Laurence Fauchelle uses this game to develop control of the mainsheet and heel.

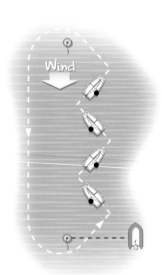

Wind

Sailing Positions Game

A great game to encourage sailors to make smooth transitions between different sitting positions without upsetting the balance of the boat. The aim is to get the sailors sailing upwind and then blow a whistle and call out the different positions they are to sit in. The key is to make the transitions as smooth as possible, as the sailor needs to be able to move like a cat around the boat.

There are six main seating positions in an Optimist.

1 Hike

2 Perch

3 Squat

4 Sit on thwart

5 Kiwi

6 Sit on the bottom

Outside Boat Tacks Game

Start with a rabbit run. The outside boat then has to sail as fast and cross as many boats as possible before tacking to leeward or ducking boats to get to the inside. It's then the next outside boat's turn.

Sailor Luke Patience, 4th Optimist Europeans and 2nd 470 Worlds, really likes this game, because the outside boat has to work really hard to try to get across the pack.

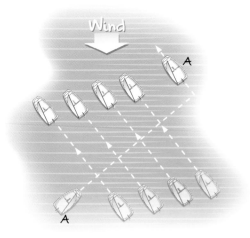

Lifted or Headed Game

Use the land or other boats to identify steady, lifted or headed. Young sailors learn a lot from this and it helps them identify windshifts.

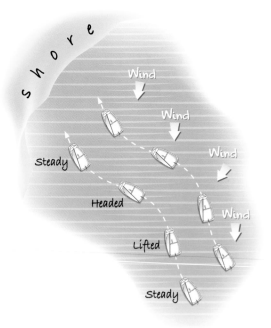

Gusts and Lulls Game

In a gust, squeeze the mainsheet, in a lull point higher. Ease the mainsheet and point lower. This is called velocity looping.

Easing and squeezing the mainsheet is an important skill to coach. The sailor needs to learn to use 1, 2, 3, 5, 10 clicks of the mainsheet block and its effect on the leech.

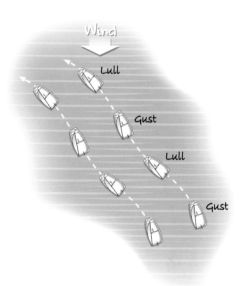

Rabbit Runs Game

There are many variations of a rabbit run. In its simplest form the fleet waits on starboard tack, and as the port tack boat crosses they accelerate under its stern and hold their lanes. The game can be played with wide or narrow lanes.

Coach Rob Wilson likes to use rabbit runs to develop steering, body movement and mainsheet control.

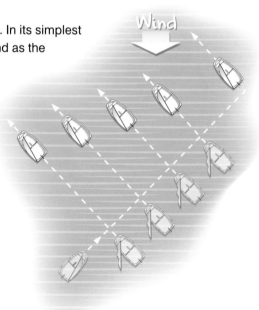

Follow the Leader and Sailing Upwind Game

A simple way of getting a group to sail close hauled.

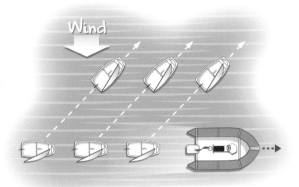

Tuning Runs Game

Tuning runs should last roughly 2-4 minutes.

- One boat remains constant. The other boat makes adjustments – but only one at a time.

- Outhaul, kicker, luff tension and sprit can all be adjusted as can the sitting position on the boat.

- Be specific and log the results.

- Measure gains or losses in half boat lengths ahead or behind, and to windward or leeward.

- If more than 2 boat lengths ahead / behind stop and start again.

½ boat length ahead

1 - 2 boat lengths apart

Bailing Upwind Game

Sailing upwind in chop. Boat has to be empty before rounding the leeward mark.

- Put 2-5 bailers full of water in the boat and then bail whilst sailing upwind.

Coach Kate Williams likes this game because less experienced sailors learn how important it is to sail with a dry boat.

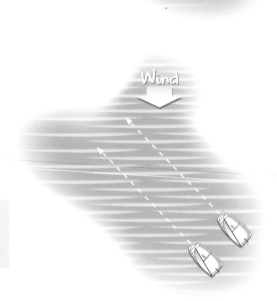

Downwind in waves

Sailors have to develop good technique when sailing downwind in waves. They need a "go for it" approach and be prepared to have a lot of fun learning and getting wet!

The difference between wallowing in the troughs and surfing down waves is huge. Young sailors must develop confidence when sailing in waves, so you should be aware that some will take longer than others to feel happy on waves.

Basic technique

1 – As a wave passes and the bow drops into the trough, the sailor needs to do one big pump and usually lean back to get the boat surfing and then sit upright once the boat is surfing.

2 – Either hold the mainsheet in, easing it gradually, or more usually in an Optimist, dump the main back out. This often kicks the boat forward – a lasso pump.

3 – Sail fast and straight, bearing away down the wave (downturn), or maybe heading up a little (upturn). The longer the sailor can stay on a wave going in the right direction, the greater the gain.

4 – The sailor needs to try to link waves together.

5 – Following the initial pump and ease or dump of the mainsheet, sailors must avoid doing another small pump on the same waves – this breaks Rule 42.

Downwind in Waves Games

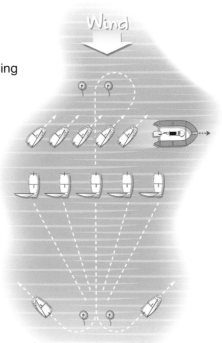

Wind

* Follow the leader into a windward mark rounding then proceed downwind

* 1 pump per wave

Remember that timing is everything.

Coach Josh Metcalfe really likes this game where he can watch and give sailors individual feedback to help them develop downwind skills.

STARTING

The ability to start well is one of the most important, as it can count for as much as 90% of a race. It is the dynamic moving part of a race. Coaching starting is great fun and the aim is to provide sailors with the confidence to use a wide range of starting skills. To have any chance of being successful sailors need a starting plan. Your role is to help the sailors develop their starting plan.

Starting Plan

- Priorities, wind, tide, geographical features.
- Steady wind or shifty wind?
- Line bias.
- Favoured side (if any)?
- Transit.
- Waves or flat water?
- Committee boat-pin boat.
- Boat set up.
- Shifty or boat speed day?
- How the sailor is feeling.
- How to deal with the effects of wind and tide.

Key priorities are:

Plan
All sailors need a starting game plan as well as a back up (Plan B).

Boat handling
Sailors need to have good boat handling skills to be able to control their boats in close proximity to other boats.

Positioning
They need to position their boats to get the best start in the area of the start line they start in.

Acceleration
Sailors have to be great at accelerating in big and small spaces.

Confidence
They have to be confident that they have the skills to get a good start under the pressure of competition.

Some other considerations

- Use a watch to get starting signals.
- A thorough understanding of where the start line is.
- An understanding of speed, timing, and distance.
- Recognising the effect of tidal streams on the start line.
- The ability to understand what is changing on the start line.

- The ability to know when the proposed start isn't going to work, and to escape early enough so that a good start can still be achieved.
- The need to have a Plan B and be flexible if the start doesn't go well.
- How to recover from a bad start.
- Be careful of Rule 42 on the start line.

Top tips

+ Developing confidence and decision making will only come from a lot of varied starting practice.

Start Games

There are many games to develop starting skills. Most start games relate directly to an actual race so start practices are an invaluable way to help a sailor develop their skills. The following games are examples of the many variations you can use.

Bias Game – To work out the bias

- Go head to wind on the start line.
- The end that is closest to the wind is the bias.

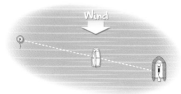

Another way to work out bias:

- Sail along the line.
- The end the sailor has to sheet in more to get to is the biased end.

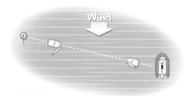

3 Pins Bias Game

Use 3 pin ends and select a different one for each start or, to make it simpler, use one pin end and lengthen or shorten the anchor line on the RIB.

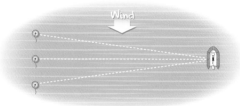

Safe Transit and Over The Shoulder Transit

These games can be used by a group
of sailors teaching them to start
in the middle of the line.

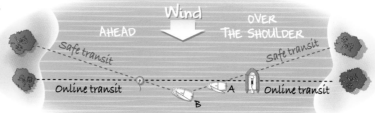

Transit Game on a Long Line

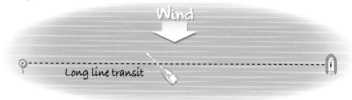

Coach Brian Staite finds this a particularly useful game
which helps sailors judge where the line is.

On a very long line, the sailor has to sail to
the middle and judge where they think the
line is by stopping and putting their hand up.
(fig 1). The coach can signal back how far
away they are with hand signals.

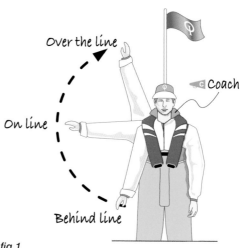

fig 1

Top tips

+ Use video to feedback the
information as it's easier for
children to see how far away
from the line they are.

Start Line Game

- Use a 2-1-GO starting sequence.
- The sailors sail upwind for 30 seconds to 1 minute and observe how they have done.

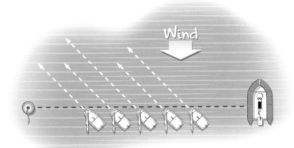

Rolling Start Game

- Set a start line with a windward mark a short distance upwind.
- Use a 2-1-GO starting sequence.
- Restart the sequence as the first boat finishes. This gives the sailor less time to get ready for the next start.

Coach Ollie Green likes this game because it keeps the sailors on their toes!

Hold Your Lane Game

I like this game because it stresses the importance of holding a lane!

- Use a simple 2-1-GO start sequence.
- The sailors have to sail on starboard for 1, 2 or 3 minutes.
- Rule – no tacking!

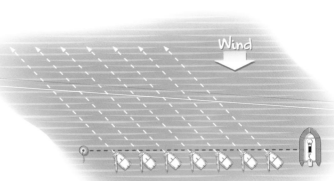

Gap to leeward Game

The aim here is for the sailor to create a gap to leeward.

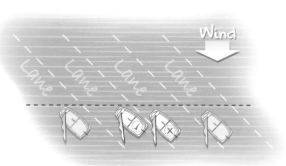

Drift Game

- Sit next to a buoy or committee boat and see how far you drift in 30 seconds or 1 minute.

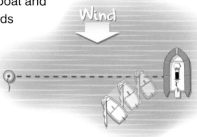

Hover and Go Game

The sailors learn to hover (hold position) on the line, using a variety of techniques to hold position.

• Double tack	• Weight forward	• Mind gap	• Slide – daggerboard up
• Stop tack	• Back the sail	• Reverse	• Hold boom
• Stack	• Sail backwards	• Scull down	• Head to wind
• Heel	• Head up	• Sheet and heel up	• Micro kinetics.
• Roll	• Bear away		
• Weight back	• Sheet in and out		

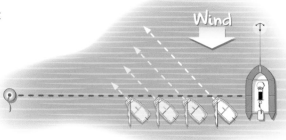

Double Tack Game

WIDE
double tack

NARROW
double tack

- A useful technique to use to move along a line.

- Start with wide double tacks, then narrow the gap down.

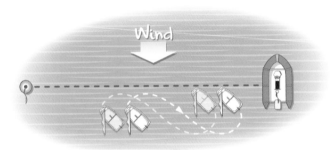

Double Tacking in a Group

Stop Tack Game

A really useful tack designed to stop the boat moving forward out of a tack.

- As the sailor goes into the tack, back the sail by pushing against the boom.

- Straighten the rudder as the boat gets to head to wind.

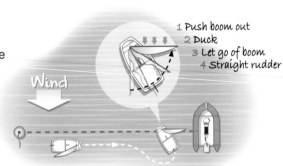

1 Push boom out
2 Duck
3 Let go of boom
4 Straight rudder

Create a Gap Game

A useful way to create a gap.

- Firstly squeeze up against boats to windward.

- Then bear away into the gap you have created to accelerate away.

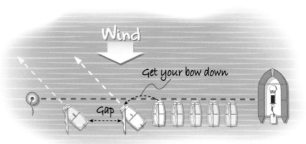

This is a favourite game of Paul Campbell-James, 8th in the Optimist Worlds, because it develops the essential skill of creating a gap.

Top tips

+ Dump the mainsheet out of the tack to stop the sail from powering up.

+ Watch out for predators who want to take your gap.

Mind the Gap Game

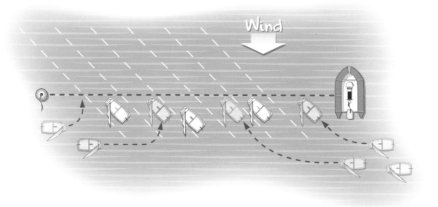

- Boats on the line create a gap to leeward.

- Boats outside the committee boat or the pin-end come in and take the gaps.

Reversing Games

Sailing backwards is a useful technique and provides a way of escaping from a tricky situation.

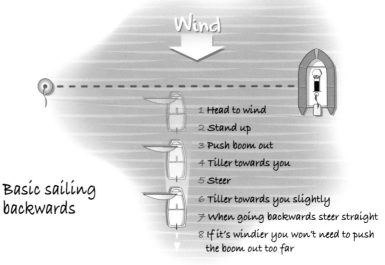

Wind

Basic sailing backwards

1 Head to wind
2 Stand up
3 Push boom out
4 Tiller towards you
5 Steer
6 Tiller towards you slightly
7 When going backwards steer straight
8 If it's windier you won't need to push the boom out too far

Remember if you are sailing backwards you have no rights.

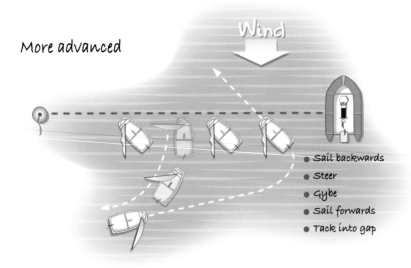

Wind

More advanced

- Sail backwards
- Steer
- Gybe
- Sail forwards
- Tack into gap

The neglected Pin End Start

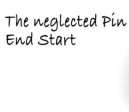
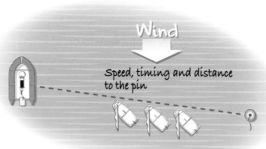

Wind

Speed, timing and distance to the pin

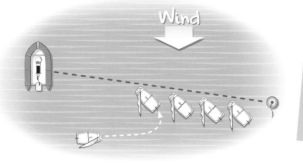

Wind

Escape From the Pin Game

Sailors can mess up a pin end start because they are too early. They panic and get a poor start. A good game is to practise escaping if too early.

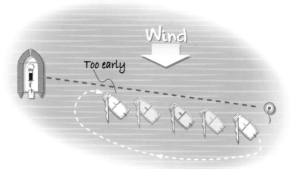

Wind

Too early

Late at the Boat End

A gap is often created at the boat end of the line. This game helps sailors to use this useful starting technique to their advantage.

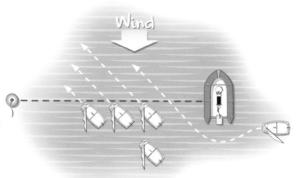

Wind

Split Start Line Game

There are many variations with
this game:

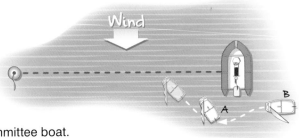

- Split the line into 3
  segments; pin,
  middle and boat.

- Split the sailors into 3
  groups then rotate them around
  the segments.

- Adjust the bias and introduce a windward mark.

- Make sure the sailors all practise the different starts.

Block the Barger Game

In this game A's job is to
prevent B coming into the gap
between themselves and the committee boat.

Big Committee Boat Game

Use two RIBs to simulate a bigger
committee boat. Better still, try to use a
bigger committee boat when practising starting.

Welsh coach Nick Sawyer likes playing this game as it simulates a bigger committee boat.

Box Start Game

Sailors have to start from within the box – this makes starting crowded and congested!

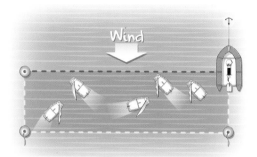

Secret Start Game

* In this game blow a whistle.

* Then, blow a second whistle anytime within the next 2 minutes to start a race.

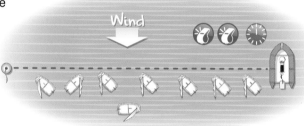

Recover from a Bad Start Game

To practise recovering from a bad start:

* Either boats B start on the first whistle and boats A start on the second, or have two start lines one above the other and all of the boats go on the same whistle.

* This is a great game for better sailors to learn to sail through the fleet.

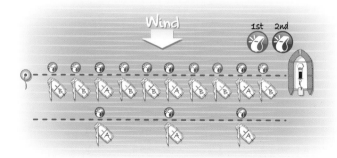

SAILING UPWIND

I have listened to many coaches joking that it is easier to say "sheet in harder" than work out how to coach strategy. Strategy is not an easy subject to coach; we can all discuss it in the classroom but getting a sailor to actually carry out their strategy on the race track is another matter. In the absence of any other boats, most sailors could carry out their strategic plan. If only it were that easy!

Three fundamentals to coaching upwind strategy

1 – Understanding the shape of the race course and the factors affecting it.

2 – Understanding how the fleet is sailing on the race course.

3 – Being able to sail a boat fast because it makes a sailor a tactical genius.

We'll now take a look only at the first two areas, as we have already looked at how to coach sailors to sail fast upwind (page 108).

Shape of the race course and the factors affecting it

It's important to make certain that your sailors have an understanding of the features which affect the race course. These features include:

• Wind direction and strength.

• Wind shifts – oscillating, persistent, or random chaotic.

• The effect of a windward shore.

• The effect of landmass which might create wind bends.

• The effect of tidal streams (current) on the race course and its effect on sea state.

This information provides a good picture of the shape of the race course.

A straightforward simple race course may at first look easy. However, these factors can dramatically affect the shape of any race course. The following examples show these effects and playing the games can be used to develop strategy to a sailor's advantage.

Top tips

'Think about your pre-race routine which will help you to start well and sail fast in the right direction.'

Ben Ainslie,
3-Times Olympic Gold Medallist.

Shore based strategy games

Simple shore based and water based games can be used to good effect ashore using whiteboards or flipcharts. Introduce factors such as tide, wind and land and get sailors to work out the best way to get upwind in the absence of any other boats.

Normal Upwind Game

A simple model which helps sailors understand basic strategy *(fig 1)*.

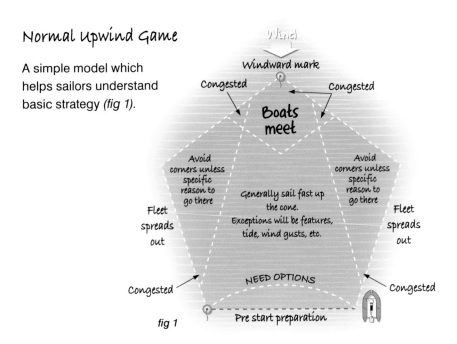

fig 1

Split Tacks Game

- A good game *(fig 2)* to see if there is a favoured side to the race course.

- Works well in stable conditions but not so well when it's very shifty.

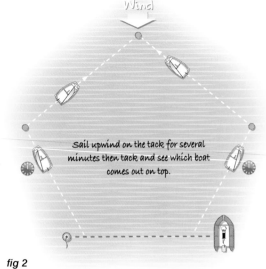

fig 2

Current and tidal streams

When you are coaching in current or tidal streams you need to think of the effects they have on the sailing and course. Think of games and exercises to help sailors develop their awareness in current.

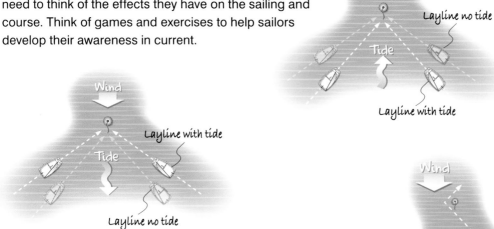

Layline no tide

Layline with tide

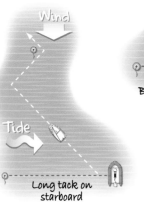

Layline with tide

Layline no tide

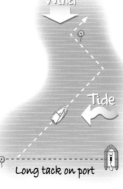

Long tack on port

Boat A will be headed and boat B will be lifted off the line

Long tack on starboard

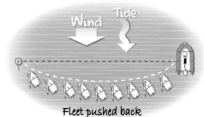

Fleet pushed back

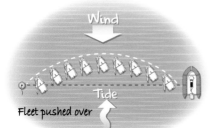

Fleet pushed over

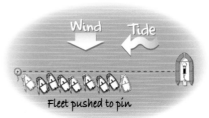

Fleet pushed to pin

Variable Windward Marks Game

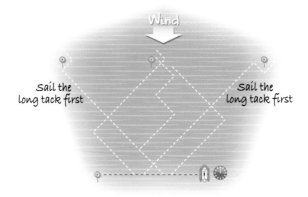

- This game keeps the sailors on their toes!

- Let them know which windward mark they are to sail to in the last minute before the start, as this helps to simulate large wind shifts.

- It's possible to make the marks even more extreme left or right.

NZL coach Andrew 'Wilzy' Wills likes this game because it makes sailors think about their priorities.

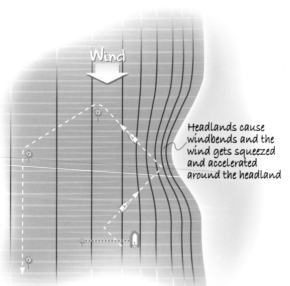

Headlands cause windbends and the wind gets squeezed and accelerated around the headland

Effects of land features

- Set up exercises to enable sailors to learn to use features.

- Good games include getting some sailors to sail into the bend and others not to use the bend.

- Sailors will soon see where the gains are to be made.

Using a compass

A compass is a very useful tool used to help sailors develop their awareness of wind shifts. There are two main types of compass:

1 – Tactical compass 0-20.

2 – Compass with a 360° compass rose.

The most important aspects of using the compass are:

- To confirm visual clues that the wind is shifting.

- On courses out to sea where there are no visual reference points.

- Be aware that a compass can be a distraction, particularly to younger sailors.

Simple ways to develop compass skills include:

Tactical racing compass

- Sail upwind on one tack and note the changes in compass heading and relative position to other boats.

- The compass can be used to identify start line bias.

Shifts, bends and clouds

Sailors need to be able to identify and use shifts while sailing upwind and understand the basic shifts.

- Random chaotic shifts.
- Oscillating shifts.
- Persistent shifts.
- Wind bends.
- Shifts caused by clouds.
- Gusts and lulls.

Spot the Shift Game

A great game is to get sailors to sail upwind in a shifty location on one tack and simply call out when lifted, headed or steady. The following games help sailors understand how shifts can be used to their advantage.

The aim of this game is to learn to use wind shifts.

- Boats A and B always have to be on opposite tacks.

- Boat A always has to be on the headed tack and boat B on the lifted tack.

- Boat B should find that they overtake boat A without trying.

- This game is best played in shifty conditions.

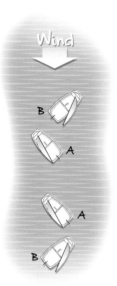

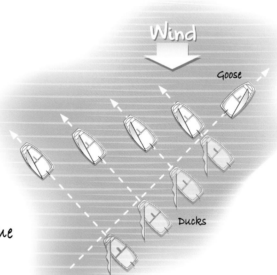

Goose and Ducks Game

- Start with a rabbit run.

- The rabbit then becomes the goose.

- The goose sails on the headers and soon the ducks will overtake him / her.

- The game is best played in shifty conditions.

 This is a favourite game of Ollie Woodcock, the GBR Windsurfing coach.

Tactics

Tactical decision making skills are an essential part of Optimist sailing and the coach's job is to help to develop those decision making skills. A simple way to think about tactical decision making is by using this grid.

Risk		+ Skill	=	Tactical Decision
Low Risk	+	High Skill	=	Easy choice
High Risk	+	High Skill	=	Winning moves only
High Risk	+	Low Skill	=	Avoid
Low Risk	+	Low Skill	=	Be careful

Tactics upwind

The start is critical in determining whether a sailor is able to carry out a plan for the upwind leg of the course. Often less experienced sailors don't get good starts and experience leading the fleet. More experienced sailors who are good at starting and leading forget how to sail in traffic and work their way through the fleet.

Even if a sailor gets a good start it's no guarantee of success at the windward mark. Sailors need to learn boat on fleet and boat on boat tactics to make sure that any early advantage is consolidated.

The following exercises and games are designed to help sailors develop their upwind tactical skills.

Start Ahead Game

A simple game which gives sailors on the front row the opportunity to practise leading.

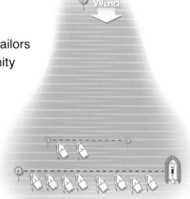

Coach Ally Martin likes this game because less experienced sailors get the opportunity to lead the fleet.

Start Behind Game

Often, better sailors forget how to sail in dirty air or through the fleet. This provides the sailors on the back line with the opportunity to:

* Find a lane
* Get onto the lifted tack
* Sail through the fleet.

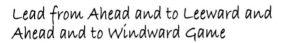

Lead from Ahead and to Leeward and Ahead and to Windward Game

* Start off with a start line and a forward start line.
* Boats A and B start on the front start line.
* After the start, boats A and B can then lead from ahead and to leeward and ahead and to windward.

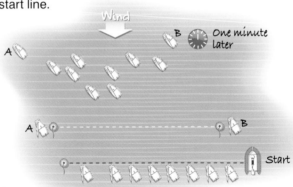

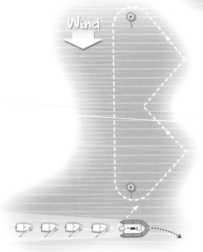

Leeward Mark Follow On Game

* Follow the leader into windward or leeward.
* The leader has a good lead and learns to defend around the course.

Coach Kirsty Bonar says this game really develops leading skills.

Boats meet upwind games

When boats are sailing upwind there are important decisions to be made. The actions a sailor will take are simple. They are:

• Duck

• Tack

• Carry on.

However, the decision making behind the action is critical, as sailors must know if they are on headed or lifted tack, whether they need to go left, right or up the middle of the course, and what the proximity to the laylines and windward mark are.

Duck-Tack-Carry On Game

The simplest of games but very important.

• Boat B, the give way boat, has 4 main options.

• It is important that the sailors learn which is the most appropriate in each situation.

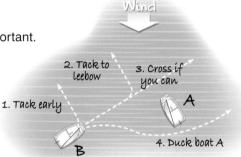

Multi Boat Duck-Tack-Carry On Game

• Use a 2-1-GO start sequence and as short a windward mark as possible.

• Half the fleet start on port tack, the other half start on starboard tack.

• The port boats' aim is to get over to the right hand side of the course to make the windward mark.

• The boats on port have to work out whether they will duck, tack or cross.

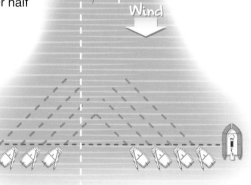

River Bank

A great tactical game.

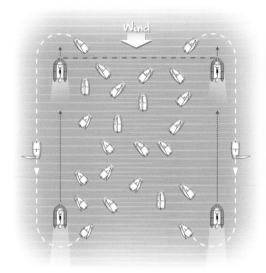

- Start the group between 2 RIBs sailing upwind.
- The group then have to sail up the river bank.
- The river can get narrower or wider.
- Boats score a point when they round the upwind RIB.
- The boats then sail around the outside and sail up the river to score again.

 I saw Danish coach Kenneth Andreasen play this game with nearly 100 Optimists in Palamos.

Cover – Break Cover Game

This game involves 2 boats.

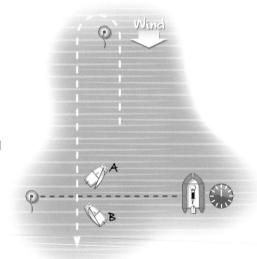

- Start with a 1-GO
- One boat starts behind the line on starboard and the other starts above the line on port.
- Boat A tries to cover boat B and boat B tries to break the cover of boat A.
- Boat A tries to get to the windward mark in the lead.
- A great boat handling and tactical game.
- You can add more boats as the game progresses.

Sailing the fleet

Sailors must understand the concept of sailing the fleet and their positioning in relation to the fleet. At the simplest level this would include:

- Keep between the majority of the fleet and the windward mark.
- Unless there is a compelling reason sail up the middle of the course.
- If the majority of the fleet go one way, unless the sailor has a guaranteed reason to go the other way, it is sensible to go with the fleet.
- If a sailor thinks one side of the course might pay, they could protect that side of the course.
- Sailors need to be patient in shifty conditions and not chase the fleet.

The following grid and games will help sailors think about their positioning when sailing upwind.

The Grid

This grid is a useful tool for a sailor or a coach to draw the course a sailor took upwind.

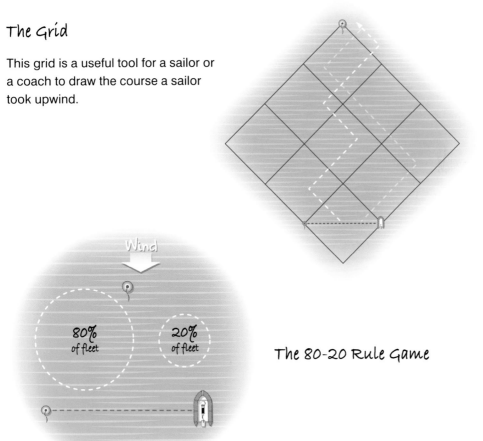

The 80-20 Rule Game

Leverage Game

In this game the sailors learn about risk and reward.

Wind

Big gain
or
big loss

Small gains
small losses

Big gain
or
big loss

Approaching the windward mark

The approach to the windward mark is an important part of the race. It is a time when the fleet comes back together and big gains and losses can be made. It is therefore essential that sailors get plenty of practice approaching the windward mark. The following games are very dynamic. With all of these games it is essential to stress the importance of rules observance and no collisions!

Rabbit Run to Windward Mark Game

This game leads to lots of tactical decisions to get to the windward mark.

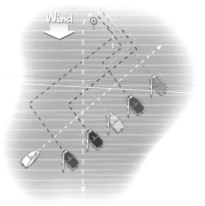

Start to Windward Mark Game

This is a variation on the Rabbit Run to Windward Mark Game.

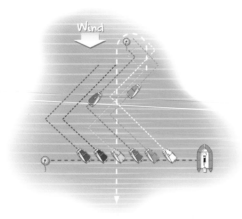

Windward Mark Mayhem Game

A great game for a large group.

- Each group gets the opportunity to approach the windward mark using different approaches.
- No collisions.

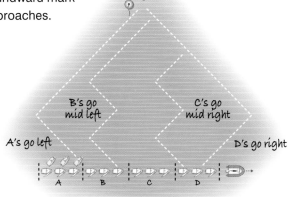

Sweet Spot Game

This game is designed to get the sailors to come back to the middle of the course below the windward mark.

- Sailors then decide upon the final approach to the windward mark.

C

This is a favourite game of coach Neil Marsden.

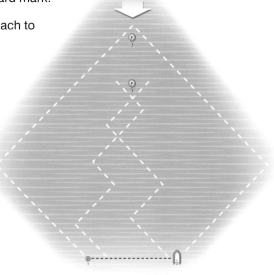

THE REACH

The reach is often a procession; however there are opportunities for gains and losses to be made. Sailors must have a clear plan of what they are trying to achieve. In many ways the main aim is not to lose any places and if possible to pick off individual boats. These games provide sailors with the opportunity to learn about different approaches to the reach.

Gusts and Lulls Game

- Sailors have to learn to head up in the lulls and bear away in the gusts to keep high boat speed.

- They need to avoid getting into a boat-on-boat battle and remember the bigger picture.

- Sailors must try to stay on waves.

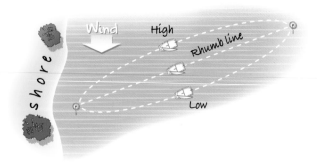

Sailing High or Low Game

Using a transit on a reach can be helpful.

- Sailors may want to sail high to get over a group or in wind with tide conditions.

- They may also want to sail low if the fleet is going high or there are wind against tide conditions.

THE RUN & LEEWARD MARK ROUNDING

In the absence of any other boats the run and leeward mark rounding are easy to perform well but as soon as other boats are involved the situation can become much more complicated. Usually in Optimist sailing the shortest route is the fastest, easy if a sailor has a good lead, but when other boats on the run start to affect the wind the fleet must spread out to get clear air, taking advantage of any wind shifts.

The main aim with the run is to make gains where possible and then gain a good position into the mark and hold your height having options after the rounding. The leeward mark rounding is one of the few places in a race where after the first beat it is possible to make significant gains.

Sailing Downwind on the Run Game

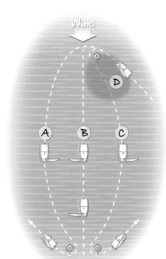

A – Sailors need to think which way they need to go up the next upwind leg.

B – Sails high but sailors must think about how to get back inside at the leeward mark, often heading up late with speed to round the mark.

C – Sails down the middle – often leading or well behind.

D – Sails low and protects the inside.

Be careful sailing too low at D because of wind shadow created by boats on the starboard layline.

Downwind in waves

Optimists will surf downwind in waves and considerable gains can be made using good technique. To become skilful downwind, sailors need a lot of practice in varying conditions. Speed and timing are essential components of good downwind technique.

* The sailor needs to be going fast enough to get onto a wave, and needs to time the pump so that it takes place just as the bow drops and the boat reaches the steepest part of the wave. Remember the racing rules permit a sailor to pump once on each wave to promote surfing so it is important to make full use of that one pump.

* The sailor then has three choices, go straight, head up or bear away. This decision depends on the shape of the wave, the positions of the fleet and leeward mark.

* Once an Optimist has picked up a wave it is usually much easier to get onto the next one, and then the next.

* Every wave lost is a gain to another boat and every wave gained is a gain against another boat. Huge gains or losses can be made downwind in waves. Optimist sailors have to develop good technique, have fun and be confident in waves.

Leeward mark rounding

The aim here is to minimize any losses and make gains wherever possible. This is a dynamic, fast changing part of a race and sailors must be aware of the changing tactical situation as they approach the mark. They need to understand the tactical impact of being right-of-way or give-way boats, being clear ahead, clear astern, overlapped and the importance of the 3 boat length zone.

They have to learn to recognise what is happening and act on it accordingly. The inside berth at the mark is a must, and slowing down to get inside is essential. Being an outside boat rounding a leeward mark is usually a disaster and leads to many places lost and fewer options being available. There are many leeward mark rounding games; using a normal race course will do, but there are some great fun games which make it a lot clearer.

Leeward Mark Rounding Game

- Sailors round the leeward mark and keep going on port until the whistle blows.
- The group then go downwind and round the next mark.
- Use a free floating leeward mark.

Approaching the Leeward Mark

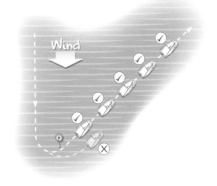

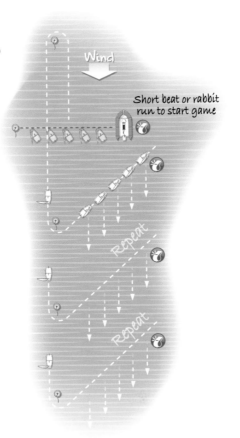

Wind

Short beat or rabbit run to start game

Repeat

Repeat

The Leeward Mark Game

- Various options to round the gate.
- Sailors need to think about which side of the course they are sailing up, and any shifts coming down to the gate.

Wind

The Gate Game

- Set one mark further to windward than the other.
- Significant gains can be made.

Wind

THE FINISH

Many places are gained or lost at the finish of a race, and yet it is probably one of the least coached aspects of Optimist sailing.

There's a lot of pressure coming to the finish and sailors must be equipped with the knowledge and experience to make the right decisions as they near the finish line. Encourage them to write down the number of the boat finishing ahead and behind, just in case their number is missed on the finish line.

The following games can help sailors to learn about finishing.

The Finish

* There is often a lot of choppy water around the finish caused by Optimists and coach boats.
* The finish line is often narrow and congested.
* Unless a sailor is near the front there is often a wind shadow downwind of the finish and on the starboard layline.
* Boats on laylines need to be careful, particularly boat A, who might not make the finish line.

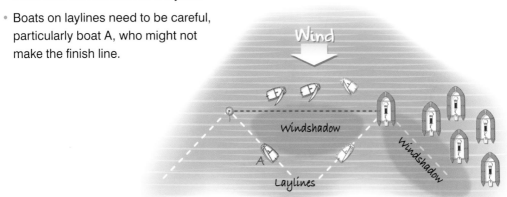

Finish Game

* Use a start line or a rabbit run start.
* Vary the bias of the finish line or use several finishing lines, calling the one you want sailors to use.

RACING

Many of the games and exercises used in this book are designed to help sailors to become skilful at sailboat racing. As Rod Thorpe put it when he made a presentation to the RYA National Coaches, "Sailors need to be great at water based chess."

Unlike many sports where the coach can communicate with the athlete during a competition, in sailing this is prohibited, and in any case the complexity of a sail boat race makes it difficult for the coach to identify the critical decisions which were made in the race. You are working to develop the independent thinking in your sailors and not a reliance on the coach. So the more you use the 'race' as the context for training the better.

The exercises and games you play need to be relevant to the development of the sailor. If they aren't, they may be good to do but what is their relevance? It is possible to run long or short races and there is a temptation to run lots of shorter races. That's fine and it has its place, however it is not quite the same as a real race. Time has to be spent training over the full race distance with windward legs of over 25 minutes. This will really develop sailors' strategic and tactical skills along with concentration and stamina.

Many race days involve being afloat for 6-8 hours, so get sailors out and practise being afloat for that time and replicate real racing with a committee boat, and a jury.

Here are some race courses you can use.

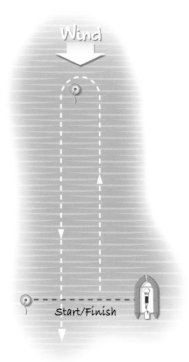

Simple windward leeward course

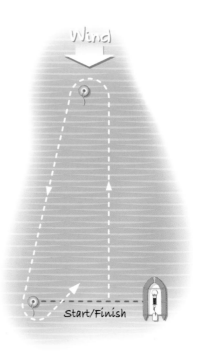

Windward leeward with a 'hook' finish

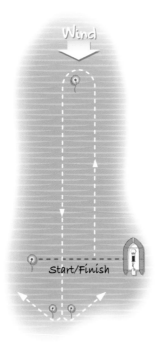

Windward leeward with leeward gate

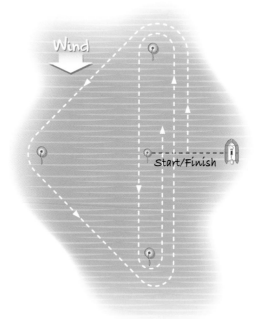

Triangular course

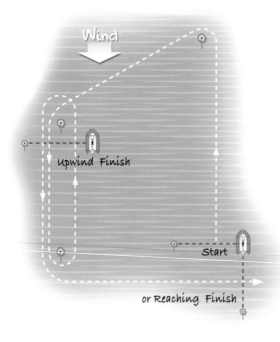

Trapezoid, inner or outer loop
with windward or reach finish

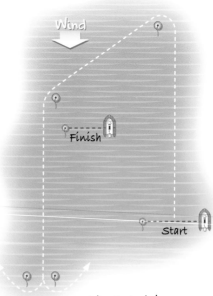

The Worlds course

COACHING THEORY

Coaching relevant theory is an essential part of Optimist coaching. The key is to make it fun, interactive, simple, interesting and into bite sized chunks.

Theory sessions requirements:

- An introduction.
- 2-3 key points which are visual and interactive.
- A summary which checks understanding.

Sailors should have a basic understanding of the following subjects:

- How a sail works.
- Weather.
- Tides and currents.
- Wind.
- Racing Rules.
- Sports psychology.
- Goal setting.
- Tying knots.

COACHING THE RULES

It's important that all sailors sail by the rules, and whilst young sailors might not know all of the individual rule numbers, they do need to know the rules that affect them. The following coaching ideas will help you to get across the rules to your sailors.

At first glance the ISAF Racing Rules of Sailing can appear to be a large piece of work. Fortunately, younger sailors need only be familiar with the definitions, part 2 rules and part 4 rules. The RYA Handy Guide to the Racing Rules makes a good introduction for young sailors.

Definitions

Sailors have to know the definitions. These cover only three pages at the beginning of the Racing Rules of Sailing – it's easy to cover these on the water and with simple quizzes.

RYA code YR1

Part 2 Rules

These are the situations which occur when boats meet. It is essential that sailors have a good working knowledge of these rules. They can be learnt by constant long term reinforcement on the water or by making them fun to learn onshore.

RYA code G80

RYA code YR7

John Doerr, a world authority on the rules, recommends breaking the part 2 rules down into 4 main areas. If you use this method it will provide a simple model for breaking down the rules when you coach them.

- Keep clear rules.
- Give room rules.
- Proper course rules.
- Avoid / don't interfere rules.
- You also need to consider tacking at a windward mark.

Ideas on how to coach the rules

Mike Hart, RYA Coaching Development Officer, says "When I'm running coaching courses, I try to get sailors thinking about their tactics and what they would like to achieve (eg being on the inside at a mark or crossing the fleet) and then to look at the rules and how they affect the desired outcome. This then introduces a rule in an interesting way rather than just looking at a rule for the sake of a rule."

The next section will provide some ideas how to coach the rules.

Exercises afloat

Set up a simple situation in which 2 boats meet. One boat is the right-of-way boat and one boat is the give-way boat.

- Then look at the tactical options each boat had.
- Work out which rules apply.
- Use real examples from the race course.

Good situations which help you to coach the rules include:

- Boats meeting upwind, port and starboard.
- Windward boat – leeward boat.
- Clear astern – clear ahead.
- Tacking.
- Approaching the windward mark.
- Rounding a leeward mark.
- Room at a mark.
- Starting.
- Finishing.

Part 3, 4, 5 Rules

Make sure that the sailors understand part 3 rules which govern the conduct of a race, part 4 rules which cover propulsion and part 5 rules which cover protests etc.

The rules onshore

It is very easy to make coaching the rules onshore very boring for young sailors. A good idea is to make any rules session interactive and visual. Keep these sessions short and just one rule at a time.

- Pick a situation which occurred on the water.

- Use a whiteboard or magnetic boats.
- Use video to emphasize learning points.
- Use quizzes to help learning.

RYA Code MBP

Walking the rules or dinghy park shuffle

Simply walk the boats around a course in the dinghy park on their trolleys and discuss the situations which occur, which rules apply and what the tactical options are.

Mock protests and advisory hearings

Mock protests are a great way to help sailors develop their rules knowledge. Take either a real situation on the water (which you may have videoed) and set up a protest hearing using the sailors as the jury and the protestor, protestee and witnesses. It's great fun.

You can also introduce advisory hearings now as part of the ISAF Racing Rules of Sailing. You can use this simple method afloat to help coach your sailors and deal with incidents as they occur on the water.

Rule 42

Rule 42 covers the propulsion rules, and in dinghy sailing it is important that all sailors understand these. The reason these rules exist is that it is possible by cheating to gain an unfair advantage over the competition. Your job as coach is to ensure that the sailors know what legal and illegal propulsion is.

A good way to make sure that sailors work within Rule 42 is to show them what they can do within the rules and make sure that they know what isn't permitted.

Prohibited actions to work on are:

- **Pumping** – repeated fanning of the sail or body pumping
- **Rocking** – repeated rolling of the boat
- **Ooching** – sudden forward body movement, often seen and used to promote surfing downwind
- **Sculling** – most often seen on the start line or in light winds
- **Repeated tacking or gybing** – most often seen in light winds.

Exceptions to Rule 42

There are a number of exceptions to Rule 42 and sailors are permitted to use the following techniques. Your job as coach is to help your sailors to develop their skills which will give them a significant advantage.

- Roll a boat to steer
- To head up or bear away, such as starting, rounding a mark or steering downwind
- Rolling a boat to tack or gybe as long as the boat does not exit the tack or gybe faster than it went into the tack or gybe
- One pump of the mainsheet per wave to initiate surfing or planing
- Scull from above close hauled down to close hauled, such as on a start line or taking a penalty turn.

COACHING AT REGATTAS

Most coaches are involved in regatta coaching, be it a small local regatta, national championship or international event. Whatever the level of event you need to ensure you are well prepared. The aim is to help the sailor to become more independent in their thinking.

Remember:

1 – Try to get sailors into a routine. Make sure they eat and drink correctly and try to reduce any stress and anxiety – focus on the event, the here and now.

2 – Most Optimist events include the sailors, parents and coach, and good communication between all three is essential. Take time to talk with parents (often anxious) as talking with them keeps them 'in the loop' and helps them cope with the event.

3 – Notice of race and sailing instructions are often complex and need checking that sailors understand.

4 – Usually equipment will have to be measured – best to make sure it is measured before the event.

5 – It is not a good idea to go to an event with any new untried sails, clothing / shoes or equipment. Sailors need to be comfortable and confident with anything new prior to an event.

6 – Regattas can be pressurised – you need to reduce the pressure on your sailors.

7 – Don't overload sailors with information, they only need enough to keep them happy and up-to-date. Some sailors won't even want to know their race results, because it increases stress – unless they win!

8 – No need for detailed wind or tidal information – each race is sailed in the here-and-now, just let them know what they need to know.

9 – Regattas often increase the level of competition, and sailors must have realistic goals. Errors on the race track often lead to large losses – particularly after the start and up the first windward leg.

10 – Many Optimist sailors are outcome driven and results focused. It is often more productive to get the processes right and the results will then follow.

11 – Starting is often harder at a big regatta than a local event and more sailors will be in contention at the windward mark.

12 – Ensure that you know your sailors. Have empathy with them. Listen to what they say and be consistent in your approach.

13 – Feedback should be simple.

14 – Try to treat a regatta as just another day.

15 – Don't forget protest time; there are more protests at regattas.

16 – If a sailor has a bad day, help them to get their perspective back. Use logic and try to minimise negative thoughts and emotions. Get the sailor to remember a good day on the water and to remember to smile!

TEAM RACING

Young sailors really enjoy team racing. It is a sport in its own right and has its own rules and tactics. It is a great way to develop teamwork, boat handling, head out of boat concentration skills and decision making skills. This short section covers some of the basics.

The course

The main course used is the ISAF Team Racing Course which is an S on its side, and a very short course. The following illustration shows how it works.

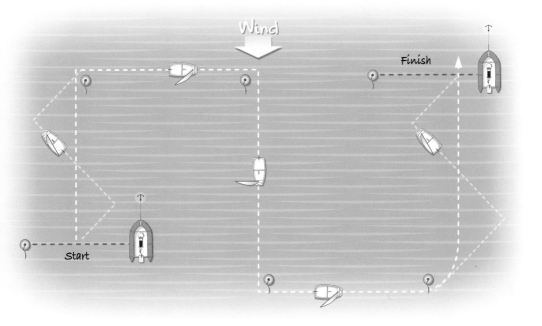

Teams

ISAF organises 3 boat team racing in the traditional format. It is also possible to run 2 boat team racing, and the Optimist Class like to use 4 boat team racing with 4 boats in each team, which Bard, the Norwegian coach, describes as 'beautiful' team racing.

Rules

The rules of team racing are mostly those of sail racing but there are some important differences which are shown in Appendix D of the ISAF Racing Rules of Sailing.

Sail fast

Often the fastest team on the water will win and sailors must sail as fast as they can unless carrying out a team racing manoeuvre.

Communication and decision making

Sailors must communicate with the rest of the team and the team needs to think ahead. They need to decide what they want to do and work out if it has a good chance of succeeding. If it does, then do it, then get back to sailing fast. If not, continue.

Team racing manoeuvres

Carry out a manoeuvre then get back to sailing fast.

Starts

Sailors must remember the starting laylines and need to avoid being forced out of the start.

Either just start well, crowd a biased end or pair up against the opposition.

Breaking a tail

If a sailor is being tailed, speeding up, slowing down, turning and other boats are a way of breaking a tail.

* Sailors need to be careful where they start.
* If they want to have a good start then zones 1 and 2 are best.
* If they are trapped in zones 3, 4 or 5 they will have trouble starting.
* If a sailor wants to trap a sailor from the other team, zones 3, 4 and 5 are the best places to do so.

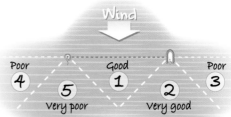

Starting

Bow down to close hauled, heel to leeward and squeeze mainsheet.

Stopping or slowing

Dump mainsheet, back main, zig zag, or luff.

Mark trap

A good way of stopping an opponent and letting your sailor through:

- Boat A slows down and traps boat B to let boat C through.

- Boat A then follows boat C.

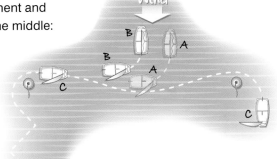

Pass Back

On a reach or a run hold up an opponent and let your sailor through, like piggy in the middle:

- Boat A slows and boat B overlaps to windward.

- Boat A luffs boat B and in doing so lets boat C through.

- Boat B then bears away to follow boat C.

Swapping upwind

This is where there are two pairs with one team leading upwind. The leader of each pair swaps and covers the opposition.

- If one team is leading two other teams, sometimes the opposition will try to come together to disrupt the pairs.

- The controlling pair can swap pairs, maintaining control.

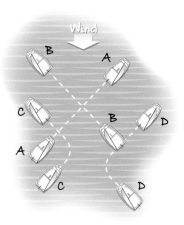

Escaping cover

Sometimes one sailor locks on to another and it is difficult to break away. Using other boats and buoys are a good way to break cover.

Strategy

It often pays to protect the right hand side up a short windward leg, and the left on the downwind legs.

Winning and losing

- If a team is winning they need to extend away and stay out of trouble and if a team is losing they need to compress the race to get back in touch.
- Many 4 boat team races are won and lost within 1 boat length of the finish line – so never give up.
- In a stable winning position such as 1, 2, 3, that team can extend and win but in an unstable position such as 1, 2, 5 and 6 the opposition will try to drive 5 and 6 to 7 and 8 and then win.

Penalties

The standard self taken penalty is a one turn penalty 360°.

If the protest is from the jury who are following and a boat does not take a penalty the jury will signal a green flag for no penalty and a whistle and red flag to the boat which has to take the penalty which will be a two turns 720°.

There are more severe penalties which can be found in Appendix 4 of the Racing Rules of Sailing.

Points

The team with the lowest score wins. If it's a draw on 18 points, the team with first place loses. Sailors must know and understand winning and losing combinations.

WORKING WITH SQUADS

Squad coaching has become very professional over the years. Often a squad will have up to 30 sailors, 4-5 squad coaches and a head coach heading up the programme.

The head coach is the main point of communication for the squad and will organise the programme and make sure the logistics are delegated and completed. Duties include arranging venues with good access to water, training rooms which have to be booked well in advance, coach boats and training marks.

Weekend sessions

Before each weekend the head coach will email the squad with the programme, aims and objectives, often working with a parent who helps coordinate the logistics.

- The head coach will split the squad into groups, usually in discussion with the squad coaches, and allocate coaches to sailors.
- Squad coaches support the head coach and also look after their own group of sailors and should be prepared to lead whole squad sessions.
- Squad coaches need to provide their group before going afloat with briefings, give feedback on the water, and a debrief on-shore.

Coaching responsibilities

Coaches have a range of responsibilities, to themselves, the sailors, parents, the national governing body and the sport as a whole. They should never do anything to bring the sport into disrepute.

Coaching children

When coaching children under the age of 18, coaches have clear responsibilities:

Loco Parentis

You have to provide the same level of care for a child as any reasonable parent.

Child Protection

Coaches working with sailors under the age of 18 have to have read and understood the Child Protection Policy detailed at www.rya.org.uk

Sample squad programme

An example of a daily programme for a squad.

Optimist National Squad – Outline programme

Weymouth and Portland National Sailing Academy

The main aims of the camp are to get ready for the autumn events and of course have plenty of fun. We'll work on:-

- Boat handling
- Starting
- Speed
- Tactics and strategy
- Racing
- You need to think about your goals for the weekend.
- Please bring the weather forecast information with you.
- Check out Portland Harbour on Google Earth.
- Please note that you will need to bring a packed lunch with you on Saturday and Sunday.
- If you can bring some post sailing snacks that would be great.
- You need fitness kit.
- You need to bring your drinkers and snacks.
- You will need sun cream and sunglasses because it will be sunny.
- Please note that it is a busy weekend at WNPSA this weekend. The main club car park will be full so you will need to use the car park on the left of the club entrance.
- You will then be able to unload boats and wheel them over towards the slipway. Please don't put the boats on the slipway as we have to keep the access to the slipway clear.

Saturday	Activity	Parents	Coaches
0930	Boats Rigged. Whole squad briefing downstairs in Club Room. Features of Portland Harbour.	Day house parents to see head coach.	Briefing at 0910 upstairs in the club.
0945 - 1000	Squad briefing. Split into groups for group briefing and goal setting. Warm up ashore.		
1030 - 1230	Boat and rig check. Boat handing in small groups. Larger group exercises. Starting. Tactics and Strategy.		
1230 - 1300	Packed lunch. Video review.		
1300 - 1700	Technical activity in larger groups followed by racing.		
1700 - 1715	Post sailing snacks.		
1715 - 1815	Change – group debriefs. Video review.		
1815	Day ends. Parents pick up sailors.		

FITNESS FOR SAILING, FOOD, DRINK & SAILING CLOTHING

Sailors underestimate how fit they need to be to sail an Optimist well. Most young sailors participate at school in a fair amount of physical education which should help provide all round fitness.

All round fitness training should include the following:

- Aerobic fitness
- Hand and eye coordination
- Strength
- Speed
- Stability
- General fitness
- Agility
- Core stability
- Balance
- A basic fitness program.

Balance and transferring weight training

On the water sailors really do need good balance and the ability to transfer weight from one leg to another.

1 – Standing on one leg is a good game. Get them to try to do it with eyes shut!

2 – Transferring weight from one leg to another by bending the leg to transfer the centre of gravity over that leg.

3 – Sitting on a chair with legs out in front, the sailor can't stand up, but by bringing their feet underneath, it is easy to stand up.

Good ways to develop sailing fitness include:

- Swimming
- Gym balls
- Rowing
- Circuit training
- Cycling
- All round school sport.

Fitness games

Apart from traditional fitness activity, there are some good agility games which can be used to develop tactical awareness using cones and space markers. Yoga exercises aid flexibility.

Nutrition and hydration

You must consider the nutritional and hydration needs of all your sailors, Optimist sailing generally isn't a highly physical sport so a good balanced diet is ideal. It is part of your job to help educate your sailors about what they should eat and drink.

Food for sailing

Carbohydrates – great fuel for sailing as they release energy. There are two types:

1 – Slow release energy is released slowly into the body's system and includes potatoes, pasta, cereal, baked beans, rice, bananas, malt loaf and jam sandwiches.

2 – Fast release energy is released quickly – 'a suger shock', and includes jelly babies, jelly cakes, fig rolls, dried fruit, cereal or energy bars and carbo drinks and Mars bars.

Proteins – Essential for developing muscles and providing minerals which keep the body working properly. Proteins are found in fish, dairy products and nuts.

Fats – Some fats are good for you and are found in fish, nuts and seeds. Other fats which aren't so good for you include fatty meat, processed meats and hydrogenated fats used in cakes and biscuits. Watch out for the amount of chips and fried food sailors eat!

Breakfast

The most important meal. Cereal, toast and fruit juices are really good but avoid full cooked breakfasts.

Afloat

Eating a little and often is a good plan.

What to drink?

Sailors quickly become dehydrated unless they drink little and often. An Optimist sailor needs to drink about half a litre to a litre of fluid an hour when out on the water.

Specialised drinks are available and it is a good idea to go for those with a lower level of carbohydrate. An alternative to specialised drinks is water with a little fresh orange juice and a small amount of salt added.

Drinking too much water can lead to more dehydration, because water flushes through the system without being absorbed, washing electrolytes out of the body.

Post race or training

- After a sunny light wind day, a sailor will not have been very active and probably will not need to replenish much energy.
- After a windy day afloat sailors will need to build up their energy levels quickly. Pasta, malt loaf and jam sandwiches will soon replace the energy used up during the day.

Sailing clothing

Sailors should always wear appropriate sailing clothing. For those who sail in hot climates all year round, shorts, T shirts or rash vests, a hat and sun cream are all that is needed. For the rest, wetsuits, dry suits, fleeces, thermals, hats, gloves and sailing boots are required during winter and a minimum of hikers and spray tops in summer.

WORKING WITH PARENTS

Coaches, sailors and parents have to work together to help sailors reach their potential. Sometimes sailors come from sailing dynasties where generations of the family have been sailors. Some will come from a non-sailing family. Coaches have limited amounts of contact time with a sailor, but parents have a lot of contact time – so parents can be a great help to a coach...

The following will help you to develop a good working relationship with Oppy parents:

- Be honest, tactful and open with parents.

- Parents need to know what is going on and buy into the programme.

- Parents are often anxious and need to understand that their child will also be anxious and in the early stages of being part of a squad needs lots of support and encouragement.

- Encourage new parents to talk with old hands who will help them understand what is going on from a parent's perspective.

- Listen to parents and acknowledge their input.

- Parents are a resource, not a threat, and don't be afraid of using their good ideas.

- Parents need standards to work to as to what is OK and not OK behaviour. I once used a yellow card red card system to manage humorously a group of fairly boisterous parents! It worked.

- Younger sailors require more support from parents and parents should be encouraged to make older sailors independent.

- Parents have to understand that they can't sail for their children, and need to manage their expectations and not put too much pressure on young sailors.

- Parents get anxious at important events. Let them know this is normal to help them with a coping strategy.

- Parents should be involved in goal setting and help ensure that sailors work on training goals.

- Encourage parents to make informed choices about equipment and understand that 99.9% of the time it will be the sailor's skills and not the boat, sail or foils that win a race.

- Before spending a fortune on new equipment parents should have a chat with the coach.

Parent Roles

Where possible parents should be encouraged to assist in a range of tasks including: race results, race committee, house parents, beach masters, launching and recovering coach boats and helping with logistics for squads.

Qualities of great sailing parents

- Helpful
- Supportive
- Consistent
- No pressure or stress
- Listener, communicator
- Not a flapper
- Doesn't talk shop all the time!
- Not too emotional

- Helps the coach if needed
- Keeps a perspective
- A sense of humour
- Copes with winning and losing
- All round good person.

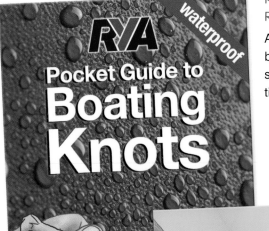

RYA Pocket Guide to Boating Knots
RYA Code G60

A selection of the most popular knots used by sailors. Waterproof and stays open so younger sailors can use both hands to tie knots.

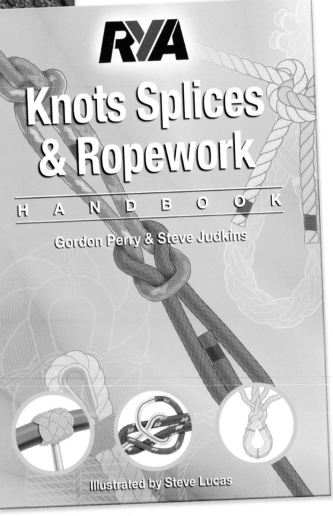

RYA Knots Splices & Ropework Handbook
RYA Code G63

The bestselling "bible" of knots, splices and ropework. Everything from the basics to the most elaborate as well as expert advice on the different types of ropes and their usage. Great as a prize!

KNOTS

All sailors need to be able to tie some basic knots; the following are a selection of the more useful knots.

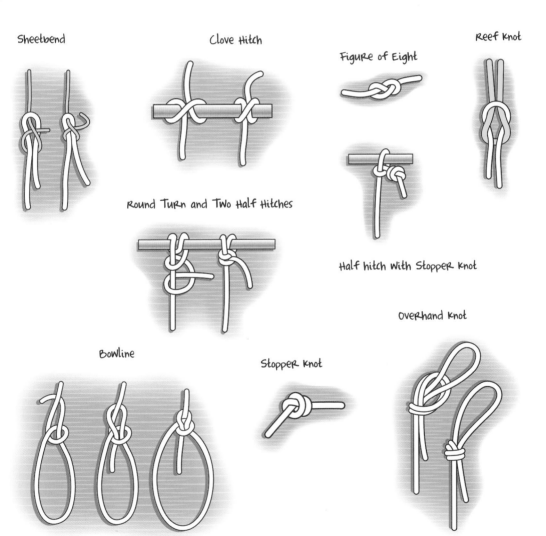

Sheetbend

Clove Hitch

Figure of Eight

Reef Knot

Round Turn and Two Half Hitches

Half hitch with Stopper Knot

Bowline

Stopper Knot

Overhand Knot

Shop online at
www.rya.org.uk/shop

gettheknowledge

- Secure online ordering
- 15% discount for RYA members
- Books, DVDs, navigation aids and lots more
- Free delivery to a UK address for RYA members on orders over £25
- Free delivery to an overseas address for RYA members on orders over £40
- Buying online from the RYA shop enables the RYA in its work on behalf of its members

RYA PUBLICATIONS

RYA Youth Racing

The RYA Youth Racing department work in partnership with the International Optimist Class Association (UK) [IOCA (UK)] to ensure a healthy, vibrant and inclusive programme of racing and race training activity is delivered in the Optimist class.

Initially this commences with club level activity within the Optimist flotillas that benefit from qualified and enthusiastic coaches and volunteers who help to develop young sailors' skills. Beyond the club, IOCA (UK) delivers regional activity through their regional representatives who organise numerous regional open training and racing events.

From there the logical step is to progress onto the national circuit and to the IOCA (UK) major events and national ranking series which culminates in the selection to RYA / IOCA (UK) National Junior and Intermediate Squads. Once sailors have a sufficient national ranking (circa top 80) they get invited to the selection trials for the Worlds, Europeans, and other selected international teams. The Optimist class has one of the most comprehensive programmes of international competition available and for young sailors who are really keen to progress, getting out on the European circuit is a fun and effective way to develop their skills.

The RYA makes an indirect financial contribution (usually direct to IOCA (UK) who administrate most of the activity) in order to minimise the costs passed onto parents. The RYA makes a significant contribution towards regional open training, the National Junior and Intermediate Squads, summer squads, girls training and the many international teams which IOCA (UK) arrange.

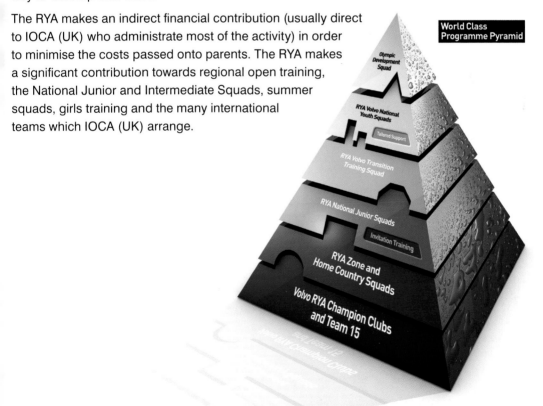

World Class Programme Pyramid

anemometer	instrument indicating wind speed
associative state	where sailor links movements with new techniques
autonomous state	where sailor automatically applies techniques consistently to a high standard
beam reach	sailing across the wind
beating	sailing in windward direction
body language	communicating through conscious/unconscious gestures and poses
bowline	type of knot
broad reach	sailing away from wind at an angle
close hauled / reach	sailing towards the wind at an angle
cognitive state	where sailor learns new movements and then has to apply them
daggerboard	retractable keel
daisy chain	method of towing several boats at once
foils	rudder and daggerboard (keel)
Google Earth	geographical satellite views website
GPS	Global Positioning System
gybing	changing direction when sailing downwind
heading up	turning head to wind
heeling	leaning the boat
hiking	leaning out to counterbalance forces on sail
hovering	holding position
ISAF	International Sailing Federation
kicker (vang)	control pulling boom downwards
killcord	attached to engine to switch off if user falls overboard
kinaesthetic learning	students who learn well through touch and movement
kiting	having sail at wide angle from boat
layline	imaginary line to a given point
leech	trailing edge of sail
leeward	downwind direction
line bias	angle at which start line differs from being square to wind
luff	part of sail attached to mast

luffing	altering course towards wind
mainsheet	main control rope for sail
mast rake	fore and aft angle of mast away from vertical
ooching	sudden forward body movement to propel boat forward
outhaul	rope system for horizontally tensioning sail
painter	line attached to bow of dinghy
pin end	end of start/finish line marked by buoy
pumping	repeated fanning of sail or body pumping to move boat forward
rabbit run	sailing in straight line on beat or close hauled
rash vest	protective vest
reaching	sailing between beating and running
RIB	Rigid Inflatable Boat
running	sailing with the wind behind
sculling	moving rudder from side to side to move boat forward
720° turn	turning in two complete circles
sheeting	action of adjusting mainsheet
shockcord	elasticated rope
sprit	small spar reaching diagonally from mast to upper outer corner of sail
tacking	sailing in windward direction on zig-zag course
TCUP	Think Correctly Under Pressure technique
telltales	pieces of material attached to sail to indicate wind flow
360° turn	turning in one complete circle
tiller	steering arm attached to rudder
transit	position judged by lining up two objects
trim	correctly balancing boat, e.g. by adopting best body position
vang (kicker)	control pulling boom downwards
VARK	Visual, Auditory, Read/Write, Kinaesthetic learning model
VHF	Very High Frequency radio
warp	line attached to anchor
weathercocking	action of wind on bows of stationary boat

Notes

RYA MEMBERSHIP APPLICATION

IT'S ALL ABOUT YOU AND THE BOATING YOU DO

One of boating's biggest attractions is its freedom from rules and regulations. As an RYA member you'll play an active part in keeping it that way, as well as benefiting from free expert advice and information, plus discounts on a wide range of boating products, charts and publications.

To join the RYA, please complete the application form below and send it to The Membership Department, RYA, RYA House, Ensign Way, Hamble, Southampton, Hampshire SO31 4YA. You can also join online at www.rya.org.uk, or by phoning the membership department on +44 (0) 23 8060 4159. Whichever way you choose to apply, you can save money by paying by Direct Debit. A Direct Debit instruction is on the back of this form.

	Title	Forename	Surname	Gender	Date of Birth
Applicant ❶					
Applicant ❷					
Applicant ❸					
Applicant ❹					

Address

Post Code

E-mail Applicant ❶
E-mail Applicant ❷
E-mail Applicant ❸
E-mail Applicant ❹

Home Tel

Day Time Tel

Mobile Tel

Type of membership required (Tick Box)

Junior (0-11)	Annual rate £5 or **£5 if paying by Direct Debit**
Youth (12-17)	Annual rate £14 or **£11 if paying by Direct Debit**
Under 25	Annual rate £25 or **£22 if paying by Direct Debit**
Personal	Annual rate £43 or **£39 if paying by Direct Debit**
Family*	Annual rate £63 or **£59 if paying by Direct Debit**

Save money by completing the Direct Debit form overleaf

Please number up to three boating interests in order, with number one being your principal interest

Yacht Racing	Yacht Cruising	Dinghy Cruising
Personal Watercraft	Sportboats & RIBs	Windsurfing
Powerboat Racing	Canal Cruising	River Cruising
	Dinghy Racing	Motor Boating

* Family Membership: 2 adults plus any under 18s all living at the same address. Prices valid until 30/9/2011. One discount voucher is accepted for individual memberships, and two discount vouchers are accepted for family membership.

IMPORTANT In order to provide you with membership benefits the details provided by you on this form and in the course of your membership will be maintained on a database. If you do not wish to receive information on member services and benefits please tick here ☐ . By applying for membership of the RYA you agree to be bound by the RYA's standard terms and conditions (copies on request or at www.rya.org.uk)

Signature

Date

Source Code

Joining Point Code

RYA

Be part of it

GET MORE FROM
YOUR
BOATING
SUPPORT THE
RYA

PAY BY DIRECT DEBIT – AND SAVE MONEY

Instructions to your Bank or Building Society to pay by Direct Debit

Please fill in the form and send to:
Membership Department, Royal Yachting Association, RYA House, Ensign Way, Hamble,
Southampton, Hampshire SO31 4YA.

Name and full postal address of your Bank/Building Society

To the Manager   Bank/Building Society

Address

                                    Postcode

Name(s) of Account Holder(s)

Branch Sort Code

☐ ☐ – ☐ ☐ – ☐ ☐

Bank/Building Society Account Number

Originator's Identification Number

| 9 | 5 | 5 | 2 | 1 | 3 |

RYA Membership Number (For office use only)

Instructions to your Bank or Building Society
Please pay Royal Yachting Association Direct Debits from the account detailed in
this instruction subject to the safeguards assured by The Direct Debit Guarantee.
I understand that this instruction may remain with the Royal Yachting Association
and, if so, details will be passed electronically to my Bank/Building Society.

Signature(s)

Date: D D / M M / Y Y Y Y

DIRECT Debit